Judaism
in America

Chicago History of
American Religion

A Series Edited by
Martin E. Marty

Judaism
in America

*from curiosity
to third faith*

Joseph L. Blau

The University of Chicago Press   *Chicago and London*

Joseph L. Blau is professor in the
Department of Religion, Columbia
University. He is the author of *Men
and Movements in American Philosophy* and *The Story of Jewish Philosophy,* among other works, and
editor of *Reform Judaism: A Historical Perspective.*

*The University of Chicago Press,
Chicago 60637
The University of Chicago Press,
Ltd., London*
© *1976 by The University of
Chicago. All rights reserved
Published 1976
Printed in the United States of
America*

Library of Congress Cataloging in Publication Data

Blau, Joseph Leon, 1909–
Judaism in America.

(Chicago history of American religion)
Includes bibliographical references and index.
1. Judaism—United States—History. 2. Jews
in the United States. 3. Zionism—United States.
I. Title.
BM205.B55   296'.0973   75-5069
ISBN 0-226-05727-5

Contents

Foreword

Jews have been Americans for over three centuries. They have been in the United States in substantial numbers for almost a century, their numbers having risen from 280,000 in 1880 to 4,500,000 in 1925; today at least 5,000,000 of them are citizens. They tend to be a historically-minded people, conscious of tradition and their tradition. They are a literate community who read and write very much. Curiously, few of their historians have chosen to write synoptic histories of their own American Jewish community.

While a set of bibliographical essays on *The Study of Judaism* which appeared in 1972 could include thousands of titles, only eighteen of these had to do with "History and Sociology" of American Jewry. The only title among these that complements this new essay by Professor Joseph Blau is a history by a sociologist, Nathan Glazer, *American Judaism*, also published by the University of Chicago Press. Lloyd Gartner spoke of Glazer's book as "a good short account. Its emphasis on the 'religious revival' marks it as a book of the 1950's." Updated in 1972, fifteen years after its first appearance, it remains a useful and treasured but isolated account.

American Jews think of themselves as a contentious debating community, who like to have more than one viewpoint made available to them for reflection and argument. And most of them tend to be aware of flux in tradition, conscious that changing times call for differing histories. For these reasons it has seemed valid to charter a new short history. Non-Jews in the historical community

must share this concept, for in a survey taken when this series of
books was conceived, few topics attracted more curiosity than did
the story of American Judaism. Professor Blau was asked to write an
essay that would combine historical narrative with reflections on the
meaning and direction of Jewish life in the United States.

Why have so few undertaken to satisfy curiosities about the
American Jewish past? The task of writing a general history
demands the competence that few share with sociologist Glazer and
historian Blau; it also calls forth a measure of audacity. Jewish
history is marked by impressive variety and internal division. It is
not difficult to tell the story of groups united by common dogma.
When dogma defines a group, historians can at least make a
beginning by consulting the textbooks that describe the boundaries
of community. While not all will agree with Professor Blau that
Judaism lacks even a common theological vision, few could disagree
with him when he observes that Jews have countless ways of talking
about their tradition and are virtually unanimous in their repudia-
tion of any efforts to impose a doctrinal system.

When a faith is held together by authority, the plot outlines are
also clear. Thus Roman Catholicism has much internal variety, but
thanks to the papacy and the hierarchy one can at least point to
borders and fences around the Catholic community. This book
makes clear that no such possibility exists in Jewry. Dr. Blau even
notes the impotence of all Jewish denominationalism: a Jewish
denomination would be hurt more than a "heretic" or dissenter,
should he or she be expelled or ostracized.

If dogma and authority are largely absent, what can be used as an
interpretive skein for telling the Jewish story in a free society? In
Blau's account one can discern that American Judaism has a genius,
a set of instincts, memories, visions, and hopes. They are not neat
or easily graspable, but a skilled interpreter can draw upon their
strands and pull them together into something coherent without
losing a sense of what William James calls "the rich thicket of
reality." This is precisely what Dr. Blau does, chiefly by the use of
four motifs.

First among these is voluntaryism. Readers will have to get used
to that spelling; it is proper, and refers to something different than
philosophic voluntarism. Depending in part upon Sidney E.

Mead's definitions, Blau shows how Jews have enthusiastically taken up one feature of American religious life. In a free and competitive society, religious and nonreligious people can be voluntaryistic. At the beginning of their religious vision they can choose a faith or no faith.

As with the beginning, so with the end. Religions which are open-ended, which are unwilling or unable to insist upon a single agreed-upon outcome, Blau calls "protestantized." By this term he is not referring to the Protestant churches, but to one of their cherished achievements or insistences. No authority can force them all to a single conclusion. American Judaism has consistently nourished this concept.

The third motif, "pluralism," has become familiar to most Americans during the past twenty years or so, ever since the gradual decline of Protestant hegemony became evident to more and more people. Pluralism was born of the legal parity assured in the American system, but this legal base has been enlarged upon in the ethos. It has forced religionists to find ways to be loyal to their own vision while coming to some positive discernments of other approaches to the sacred or of the choices not to regard the sacred positively.

Finally, in a free society the religious groups have been called upon to advertise themselves less ritually and more morally. Jews have felt at home with this final motif, for moral concepts are at the heart of their historic vision. But Professor Blau goes a step further and shows how Jewish moralism has given rise to a community that is larger and more inclusive than that presided over by the synagogues and other religious institutions. Jewish moralism has provided still another way of being Jewish; while it leads to some diffusion of community, it also calls upon many legitimate aspects of Jewish memory and hope.

One of the most attractive features of this narrative and reflective essay is Blau's unwillingness to see Judaism defined only by non-Jews, by a sometimes hostile environment. Hostility there has been, but he shows how anti-Semitism on any grand scale came quite late in North America. He does not see that it determined or provided the boundaries for Judaism, though it may have helped Jews unite in defense or in promotion of some causes. The fact that he does not rely on anti-Semitism to provide a plot for his outline of American Jewish history points to the success of his attempt: he does deal with the internal dynamics of this complex history of a people.

The result of his discernments and achievements is a history that need rely on neither stereotypes nor straitjackets. Blau instead writes open-ended history. When something new appears on the scene as it did with Zionism or the rise of Israel, he shows how it altered Jewish consciousness and destiny. The story is unfinished. But Blau has pointed to a context for the future, a map of a territory across which an unsettled people has wandered and where they have begun to find a place.

Martin E. Marty
The University of Chicago

Preface

Many books and articles have been written, by competent historians and sociologists, about the *Jews* of the United States. In discussing the Jews, these writers have found it essential to their narratives and their analyses to write about Judaism in the United States. Their primary focus on Jews has been valuable to me in my own studies, and I should here express my gratitude to Oscar and Mary Handlin, Nathan Glazer, Marshall Sklare, and Charles S. Liebman for the use I have been able to make of their work.

My own essay, set forth in these pages, is different. I have centered my attention primarily on what has happened to *Judaism* in the United States. Needless to say, since Judaism and Jews are terms of mutual involvement, I have found it necessary to write also about the Jews. I have tried, however, to keep in the forefront of my treatment the question of the impact of the American experience on Judaism. If, from time to time, I sound like a historian or a sociologist, the reason is that a historian of religions cannot avoid transgressing academic boundaries. Abstract as its ideas may be, and transcendent as its focus, any religion exists concretely in a setting constituted by time, place, and community.

The theories and interpretations presented here are the products of many years of reflection. Bits and pieces have been presented in draft form before various groups, and some sections of my text are revised from previously published articles. To all those who listened to the papers, read the articles, and gave me helpful comment and criticism, I owe my thanks.

For the past thirty years, it has been my delight to offer for both undergraduate and graduate students in Columbia University and Barnard College a course on the history of Judaism. Many of the ideas first expressed in this course have become the foundational principles of this book. In a sense, then, my students are my unnamed coauthors. To all of them, past and present, I dedicate this work with love.

No acknowledgment of mine would be complete without the attempt to find an adequate way to say what Eleanor has meant to this book and its author. Without her help, her encouragement, her devotion to my work as to her own, the book would not be here. She is, in truth, an *eshet hayil,* a woman of valor.

J. L. B.

Elizaville, N.Y.
July 1975

1 *Introduction*

Toward a Theory of Jewish History

None of the major religions of the world can be simply defined. The very factors that make them *major* religions lead to difficulties of exact characterization. For any religion is a complex of beliefs asserting one possible interpretation of the ultimate nature of the world and of the place of human beings in the world, together with patterns of practice expressing and reflecting, at least approximately, that view of the world. A major religion is one that has persisted through time, that has attracted adherents in relatively large numbers, and that has spread far and wide over the face of the earth. Persistence through time requires a religion either to have accepted and adapted current scientific or common sense views of the nature of the world or to have satisfactorily adjusted the conflict between its traditional cosmology and current knowledge and belief. To attract and hold a large number of adherents in a variety of places and times, under a range of political and cultural conditions, a religion must be flexible enough to serve as a guide, yet rigid enough to set a pattern for living.

True, there may be periods in the history of any religion in which, in a particular cultural area of the world, only negligible variations occur. But if we shift our attention to a century earlier or later or to synchronous manifestations elsewhere in the world, it again becomes clear that man's religions, particularly those called major, are constant chiefly in the ways they adapt to novel conditions. The symbols of a religion may remain unchanged, but the meanings they bear, the interpretations put upon them, the understandings conveyed through them are ever in flux. We might even say (adapting Heraclitus' words) that no man can enter the same church twice, for both the man and the church will have changed in the interval.

This generalization, unpleasant though it may be to traditionalists, is especially valid for Judaism. The reason is that there have been fewer periods of relative calm in the history of Judaism than in the history of other major religions. The wandering Jew may be only a legend, but wandering Judaism is a fact. No matter at what point in the history we start to use the name "Judaism"— whether with Abraham, or with Moses, or with the Babylonian Exile, or with Ezra, or with the rise of the Pharisees, or with the second destruction of the Temple—the record is one of unstable living conditions and an insecure people, moving about in seminomadism or being shifted from place to place by the changing fortunes of empires. With each change of cultural scene, new varieties of Judaism were developed, each one incorporating some part of the age-old traditions of the people called Jews and some part of the culture and traditions of their environment of the moment. The history of Judaism is a glorious history of creative cultural synthesis.

Thus far in this account, stress has been placed on the shocks and crises internal to Jewish history. In addition to such occasions for the adaptation of Judaism, there have been times when the culture of the whole Western world has been in upheaval, and the Jews, as a part of that world, have shared in the universal crisis of the times. The religions of the Western world, Judaism included, have had to seek a novel adjustment to new conditions or to disappear. Many religions did not have the vitality to adjust as the world changed and have disappeared as living faiths. Judaism has not disappeared; it has repeatedly proved its adaptability and flexibility and thus its right to rank with the major religions.

For reasons suggested above, the question "What is Judaism?" cannot be answered by a precise definition. No person and no group of persons has the right to pronounce authoritatively on what Judaism is, today in the United States of America, or at any other time or place in its history. There is no criterion within Judaism for orthodoxy or heterodoxy. The only way to answer the question is by an enumeration and description of varieties. In present-day American Judaism—and I should say, though many Jewish historians would disagree, in the Judaism of all times and places—there are a number of traditions that differ considerably from each other. The adherents of each of these traditions call their own version "Judaism," and sometimes deny the right of others to the name. In addition, both in the general community and among Jews themselves, "Judaism" is used as the name of the class constituted by these various traditions. Judaism, then, is a name for the many expressions of the spiritual life of those men and women in any place and at any time who regard themselves as Jews. Instead of using one form of Judaism as a Procrustean standard for the spiritual life of the Jews, we must use the multi-faceted spiritual life of Jews as the standard of Judaism.[1]

I am *not* asserting that the many versions of Judaism today do not look back upon a common tradition, both literary and historical; I *am* asserting that that tradition itself is not now, and was not at the times of its expression, a monolith. I am *not* asserting that there is no set of symbols common to all the varieties of Judaism—God, Torah, the people Israel, the Holy Land, the Messiah; I *am* asserting that the relative values, the weights assigned to these symbols, differ from age to age and from place to place and, in any one age and place, from group to group. I *am* asserting that the divergent interpretations placed upon these symbols are precisely what has enabled Judaism to survive the repeated shocks of Jewish history within world history.

The assumption, made all too frequently by Jews as well as non-Jews, that there is one and only one classical form of Judaism is altogether false. There has never been a time in the long history of the spiritual life of the Jewish people when differing varieties of Judaism have not coexisted. There has never been a single universal authority or authoritative body competent to fix the norms of belief or of practice. The Babylonian and Palestinian Talmuds do not always agree; and Babylonia and Palestine are only two among many centers of Jewish life in the early centuries after the second and final destruction of the Temple. Even the great authority of the Babylonian Talmud (which, we must remember, was less a monolithic body of laws than a compilation of multifarious precedents and traditions) was not universally accepted. And we might note, in passing, that one sentence in the Babylonian Talmud gives the broadest possible definition of a Jew: "He who renounces idol worship may be called a Jew" (Megillah 13a). There were anti-Talmudic strains in Jewish life. The medieval movement of the Karaites, born within a Middle Eastern environment closely akin to that which gave birth to the Babylonian Talmud, includes several varieties of this anti-Talmudic strain. To use Horace Kallen's phrase, which has unfortunately become somewhat hackneyed, Jewish life has always manifested "cultural pluralism."[2]

Yet this is not the whole story. For each of the variant interpretations of Judaism, in the time and place of its occurrence, is not merely a random emergent, born of the vagrant thought processes of some charismatic eccentric. It is, rather, the result of an unconscious desire to make the age-old tradition of Judaism sustain a revitalized relevance to the particular conditions of that time and that place. The differing interpretations of any one age are, in effect, competing claims on the part of their proponents to be able to serve their adherents most effectively as guides to living. To serve effectively, an interpretation of Judaism must demonstrate its capacity to focus some aspects of tradition on a current context.

The Crisis of Modernity

Since the late eighteenth century, the Jews of Western Europe and the United States of America have been living through a crisis. To a lesser degree and for a more limited period of time, the Jews of Eastern Europe have faced a similar crisis. This crisis of modernity may be the most significant of all the critical epochs through which Judaism has lived, because it is marked by the need to adjust simultaneously to both external and internal changes.

Externally, the period starting in the late eighteenth century is by and large one in which the political and economic barriers between the Jews and the peoples among whom they lived have tended to be eliminated. The Jews have been emancipated, have become "citizens" rather than "resident aliens." Public careers that were previously closed to Jewish talents have opened up—not everywhere at the same speed, but almost everywhere to some extent. Secular education is far more readily available to Jews than ever before. Even

advanced professional training is far more open; the past forty years
have seen the virtual disappearance of the *numerus clausus* in
European universities and of the equivalent "Jewish quota" at
American universities. In the culture of many countries, the
twentieth century has been marked by a centrality of the Jewish
literary figure. Jews have come to great prominence in the sciences,
and even in engineering, which, fifty years ago, was regarded as a
field not open to Jews. These past two hundred years might be
described as the time in which the Jews have come out of the ghetto
and into the world—and have done so by invitation, because, in
the world into which they have come, men are judged, by and
large, by their individual achievements and not by such factors as
ethnic origin or religion, which the modern world in theory
considers irrelevant most of the time. Needless to say, there is not
the same openness in the social world as there is in the economic,
scientific, or political worlds. The new, relatively open society
places the burden of proof on the individual; individual Jews no
longer compete only against their fellow Jews, and only for the
more prominent places in the small, enclosed community of Jews.
Now they are in competition with non-Jews as well.[3]

Internally, the discovery of the modern world has meant taking a
fresh look—reinforced by the modern physical and social sciences,
and grounded in contemporary concepts of intellectual methods
and Western notions of aesthetics and morality—at Jewish tradition
itself. This is often referred to as a crisis of Jewish identity; but such a
description makes the whole problem one of individual response. It
suggests that now, as each American Jew lives the greater part of
his life outside of the Jewish tradition, he must inevitably question
the remaining fragmentary relation that he has to the Jewish
tradition.

This element of the problem should not be underemphasized.
Only a few years ago, *Commentary* magazine polled a group of
younger Jewish intellectual leaders on the question of what influence their Jewish background, their relation to the Jewish heritage,
had had on their development. Overwhelmingly their answer was
"little" or "none." But the very lack of influence points up the
social or communal problem of the contemporary crisis in Judaism.
For in earlier days the most talented, the most able—the potential

and actual leaders among the Jews—had to find outlets for their
talents within the Jewish community. Their strength reinforced the
Jewish community. As potential leaders increasingly find the field
for their talent outside the Jewish community, internal leadership
falls into the hands of less able, less original, and less inspiring
persons. At the very time when the most gifted are needed for
reshaping the Jewish tradition to the modern world, their energies
are to a very large extent directed elsewhere. In every previous
period of Jewish crisis, there were leaders of genius to guide the
perplexed. Today's reformulation of tradition must be accomplished more democratically. The democratic experience of the
Jewish group in America can serve as a model for Jews all over the
world, not to be followed slavishly but to learn the techniques of
democratic reconstruction.

The people who have suffered, at least as much as any other
people in the world, from the conditions of life created by
totalitarian governments, especially in Central and in Eastern
Europe, should clearly be the first to reject totalitarianism and to
receive warmly the notion of a pluralistic, diversified, democratic
model for Jewish life. This would certainly be the case if human
beings were as rational in judging their own situation as they are in
judging the affairs of others. But, of course, human beings are
most irrational precisely at the point where they are themselves
most involved. In our own time, when the crying need is for the
proposal and experimental practice of as many divergent forms of
Jewish life as possible, pressure for religious uniformity has been
exerted within the Jewish world in the United States as well as in
Israel and in England and elsewhere.

In the United States, from 1840 to the present day, many
attempts have been made, all unsuccessful, to introduce an overarching form of communal control. They have failed because in
every case there were enough advocates of diversity who recognized
that the surest way to destroy the creative force in Judaism was to
establish one pattern as a touchstone of Jewish identification. Much
has been said, and will be said, about "*the* Jewish tradition." But
if the preceding brief historical resumé is at all accurate, no one
group has possession of "*the*" Jewish tradition. It might be better
if we became accustomed to talking about "the traditions of the
various Judaisms."

What's "American" about American Jewry?

Now that the Jews of the United States of America have become the largest Jewish group in Diaspora,[4] it is appropriate to question the ways in which the cultural and religious life of the people of the United States has affected the Jewishness of American Jews. It may be too early for a definitive answer. Although some Jews have been in a position to be affected by American culture for more than three hundred years, the bulk of contemporary American Jewry is composed of immigrants and their descendants since 1880, a period of less than a century. It is surely worthwhile to attempt to point out trends, however.

I take it as proven by Jewish historiography that there has been such an influence from the host culture whenever in the past a Jewish group has lived for any considerable period of time in a non-Jewish environment. That is to say, such terms as "Babylonian Jewry," "Spanish Jewry," "Moroccan Jewry," and "East European Jewry" are not merely convenient geographical labels. These terms stand for real and specifiable differences in the total complex of Jewish belief and practice. It is then proper to infer that sooner or later the process of differentiation must produce "American Jewry." The analysis here presented is limited to the differentiations. It asks only the question, "How have the patterns of American culture and religion been reflected in American Jewry?" or, in the words of the section title, "What's American," rather than what's Jewish, "about American Jewry?"

An outstanding recurrent trait in American culture seems to me to be a strong dislike for intellectual systems. Business and industry proclaim efficiency as an important advantage of their "system" while many intellectuals reject the advantages of system in philosophic, religious or political matters. In this respect as in so many others, Emerson spoke for America when he asserted that "a foolish consistency is the hobgoblin of little minds."[5] For it seems to be precisely the consistency of systematic thought that upsets so many Americans. Whether we look to Emerson himself, or to Jefferson, Lincoln, William James, or any national administration, the most cursory examination makes it clear that the value of intellectual consistency and coherence is characteristically denied. It is this rejection of consistent systematic thinking that leads to what

William James called the "open-endedness" of his own philosophy. John Kouwenhoven has traced this open-endedness in certain aesthetic matters, like America's skyscrapers, the cities that grow in America, Walt Whitman's poetry, Mark Twain's stories, and American jazz. Like sectional furniture, he pointed out, these representative American achievements are always complete, but never finished.[6]

To what Kouwenhoven said, I should like to add the important qualification that, for a large part of American cultural history, the openness has been at both ends. Dean Frederick J. E. Woodbridge of Columbia University is reported to have used the image of the hollow tube open at both ends to describe the nature of man. However appropriate the image may be for a theory of human nature, it seems to me to be the most completely accurate and vivid symbol for American thought; it is open both as to beginnings and as to conclusions. It is not merely that American thinkers, by and large, shrink from rounding out the implications and inferences to be drawn from a limited set of assumptions—not merely that they are open-ended toward the future. The assumptions themselves are unlimited, various in origin, widely regarded as of equal validity, and often mutually incompatible; American thinkers are open toward the past as well as toward the future.

In both directions, the American distrust of intellectual system has had a characteristic religious expression. I shall call these religious expressions "protestantism" and "pluralism." The term "protestantism" has been adopted to describe that movement in religion in general (not only in Christianity) which allows of a multiplicity of conclusions. "Pluralism" is often used as if it were a synonym for freedom of religion, but here it is used as the religious manifestation of the view that all starting points are equally valid. That is to say, "pluralism" means openness as to beginnings, while "protestantism" means openness as to conclusions. What I am here calling "protestantism" is what Sidney Mead has called "denominationalism."[7] In any case, "pluralism" seems to be the basis for interfaith or multifaith activity, which is so much more of a commonplace in America than anywhere else in the world that it might well be called the most characteristically American of all American religious practices. "Protestantism," on the other hand, is the principal foundation, as well as the foundational principle, of the denominational Protestant churches, to the number of some two hundred and fifty, which are distinguished from one another by their drawing different conclusions from the same—or indiscernibly different—starting points. Of recent times, contemporary Protestant Christian thought has worked out the pattern of the ecumenical movement, which asserts the community of all Christian churches despite their differences in conclusions. The ecumenical movement seems to reinforce the use of the term "protestantism" here to mean the denial of the values of consistency, or system, with respect to conclusions.

A second major, and related, trait of American cultural life is a concern for immediate practical consequences. It is in large measure this concern that diverts attention from long-range theoretical conclusions, and therefore from a concern for consistency. This might be called "pragmatism" in the sense that William James intended, although for James the practical consequences did not have to be immediate. We do not have to look to William James, however, or even to recent times, for evidence of the trait. We can find it early in the eighteenth century in Cotton Mather's *Essays to Do Good* and in Jonathan Edwards' concern for the practical fruits of Calvinistic "election" in his *Treatise Concerning Religious Affections*. Benjamin Franklin manifested the same trait in the context of secular benevolence, and many other leaders in philanthropic activity have followed in Franklin's secular path. We need look no farther than the *Federalist Papers* to find Hamilton, Madison, and Jay showing greater concern for practical political consequences than for systematic political reasoning. Indeed, there is more of the "spirit of system," however crudely expressed, in the anti-Federalist documents than in the *Federalist Papers;* yet the anti-Federalist writings are all but forgotten, while the contribution of Hamilton, Madison, and Jay is not only remembered but even regarded as one of the very greatest American contributions to theoretical political thought.

The religious manifestation of this widespread and persistent American concern for practical consequences seems to me to be the prevalence of what, in traditional theologians' language, is called "moralism." This might be defined as the tendency in religious

life to evaluate individual conduct in terms of the relations of man
to man alone, without regard to ulterior considerations of the
relations of man to God. In effect, more practical and immediate
consequences of religious commitment are substituted for more
theoretical and remote consequences as criteria for estimating the
chances of salvation. Moralism is reflected by the insistence on the
question "Does N. lead a good life?" as a prevalent American
substitute for the question "Does N. lead a Christian life?" The
distinction between moralism and religion was well understood in
America in early colonial times, and it is well understood in many
parts of Europe today. The measure of the extent to which moralism
has been carried in contemporary America is that, except to
professional theologians, the distinction between morality and
religion is today unimportant, and virtually nonexistent. To lead a
good life, to be, as Samuel Hoffenstein once put it satirically,

> . . . kind to women, children, worms
> To speak of God in the highest terms,
> To help spell words like "tetrahedral,"
> To show respect for a cathedral . . . [8]

is all that Americans generally mean by being religious. And when,
as in some recent theologies, the ancient distinction between sin
and evil is insisted upon,[9] it is greeted as a familiar acquaintance by
other theologians, but it makes no sense to the American people.

But for the sort of "goodness" that this interpretation of religion
regards as essential, churches are unnecessary, although they may
be helpful. A man or woman can be "good" without ever
attending a church or reciting a prayer or receiving a sacrament. In a
moralistic society, the churches have no special reason for being, no
unique function, and so they tend to duplicate the functions of
other organized groups of a social, fraternal or benevolent nature in
order to give themselves something to do, in order to justify their
existence. The churches themselves subordinate their proper religious functions to their adopted moral functions, and thus they
reinforce the already prevalent moralism of the society.

A third pervasive trait of American cultural life that merits
attention is what might best be called its anarchism; because of the
overtones that this otherwise useful word has acquired, we had

better follow Sidney Mead and others in calling it "voluntaryism."
This trait rests on the belief that the rights of the individual always
should take precedence over the rights of society; alternatively
formulated, that an individual's duties to himself should always
come before his duties to society. In order to hold such a belief, one
must, consciously or unconsciously, accept the Jeffersonian view
that each generation reconstitutes society and owes to the past no
obligation to transmit its heritage. Where each generation is
understood as creating society anew, every individual has the right
to select, out of the wide range of possible ways of cooperating with
his fellows, whichever way or ways he wills. Thus individual will
(*voluntas*) becomes the basis of association, instead of tradition or
heritage. All association is voluntary.

In American religious life, the voluntary principle has been taken
to mean two things. First, it has been taken as the principle of
freedom *of* religion. No governmental agency may impose any sort
of religious association on the public, nor may it coerce the
individual into affiliation with any religious association. Second,
and for our present purpose more important, it has been taken as
the principle of freedom *from* religion. Since all association is
voluntary, an individual who does not will to associate with any
religious group must be left to his isolation. Voluntaryism breaks
down completely if it does not provide room for voluntary non-
association as well as for voluntary association, for voluntary
nonconformity as well as for voluntary conformity. It is my
conviction that the combination of these principles—voluntaryism,
pluralism, protestantism, and moralism—is what makes it perfectly
possible for an American to shift his affiliation from church to
church with every shift in his economic or social status or with every
move from neighborhood to neighborhood or town to town, and
still to be regarded as a religious person if he leads a reasonably
moral life—that is, if he restricts his acquisitiveness to conventional
business channels, marries his wives seriatim rather than simultaneously, participates in some sort of social uplift movement and,
generally, keeps within the limits prescribed by law.

Is there any sense in which it is legitimate to speak of American
Jewry? To the extent that such a term as "American Jewry"

suggests a unity of belief or action, there is nothing that corre-
sponds to the term. There are a fairly large number of Jews in the
United States. They or their forebears have come to the United
States from many different lands. In each of these countries of
origin, there was developed at least one, and sometimes more than
one, novel synthesis of traditional Jewish belief and practice with
the culture of the country that was their host. Even those Jews who
came to America from countries that abutted on each other brought
with them customs that had developed differently in their various
host environments. These included such externals as customary
dress and manners but went beyond externals to matters of religious
ritual. The Jews from some of the larger European centers like
Poland brought local variations that had grown up in particular
localities, like Warsaw or Minsk, as well as their generalized
variations, the customs (*minhag*) of Poland. They formed synagogues and social groups in America in accordance with their
varying European backgrounds. For a generation, at least, they
avoided what they regarded as "intermarriage," that is, the
marriage of a boy of, perhaps, Polish-Jewish background to a girl of
Lithuanian-Jewish ancestry. Furthermore, the Jews who came to the
United States did not all arrive at the same time, and what they
brought with them in the way of cultural baggage differed
according to the time of their arrival. Jews from Germany who
reached America in the 1830s and 1840s, for example, brought
with them a different combination of Jewish and German cultural
and religious ideas than did those German Jews who came to
America in the 1930s and 1940s. Even the image of America that
each group brought with it differed. While America was a haven to
all these different groups, the pattern of American cultural and
religious life fused differently into the synthesis that each group
had as its original equipment when it landed in America. To the
extent that residues of these various cultural heritages still keep the
Jews of the United States from becoming a unity, it is improper to
speak of an "American Jewry."

Again, a "Jewry" can be created by pressure from outside the
Jewish group, as well as by developing unity within. In medieval
Germany, the customary law of the land provided no real place for
the Jews. They had yet to be kept alive for theological reasons as

well as for their services to commerce. So a special niche was created for them, the so-called Jewry-law, giving the Jewish group a corporate status outside of the regular channels. In medieval "status society," a man who was not attached to some corporate entity was helpless; he was as if he did not exist. The special law gave a quasi-official position to the leaders of the Jewish community and thus put into their hands an extremely valuable weapon for dealing with recalcitrant members of their group. Furthermore, in the late Middle Ages, residential quarters for Jews were, in many places, officially limited to an assigned sector of each town. In these *ghetti,* social pressure from one's neighbors acted as a powerful stimulant to conformity. Here is a clear example of the possibility of creating a unified "Jewry" by a combination of pressures from outside and from inside the Jewish group. One of the definitions that Webster assigns to the word "Jewry" is *ghetto.* In the United States, the legal conditions to produce a "Jewry" in this sense have never existed; and although many, perhaps most, Jews have always chosen to live in close proximity to their fellow Jews in American cities, there has never been any official designation of a Jewish quarter, even in early New Amsterdam. If in an unofficially constituted Jewish residential section, pressures to conformity have grown too uncomfortable for any individual, he has been able to move freely into another section and thus rid himself of the incubus.

Thus, the only remaining use of the term "Jewry," one that Webster notes as obsolete, seems to be the most valuable for our purposes; "Jewry" may be used as equivalent to Judaism. Judaism, as we have seen, cannot be precisely defined. It is basically not a creedal religion and has, therefore, no normative form. It is significant in this connection that the one important attempt to pin a normative form upon Judaism was the work of a non-Jewish student of comparative religion, Professor George Foot Moore of Harvard University.[10] Since there is no creed or form of subscription, it might be better always to use the word "Judaism" in the plural to indicate the absence of a standard of orthodoxy and heterodoxy. Used in the singular, it must be taken as a collective term denoting the varieties of beliefs held and practices followed by all those people in a given time and at a given place who identify themselves as Jews. If we can talk about Jewry as meaning what Jews there and then, or Jews here and now, believe and do, then we have finally isolated a meaning for the word that is applicable in the American context.

It is worthwhile to insist, with Horace Kallen, upon the element of self-identification in determining who is a Jew and, therefore, whose beliefs and practices are to come into the account. If we leave the identification to non-Jews, then we encourage racialist criteria like the Nuremberg laws; we encourage the use of ethnic rather than religious differentiae. We cannot, on the other hand, leave the identification to "other Jews," that is, we cannot say, "A Jew is one who is recognized as a fellow Jew by other Jews," because prior to setting forth criteria of identification there is no one of whom we may say categorically, "He is a Jew." Again, we should not accept the criteria set forth by particular synagogal groups; this would lead to our taking a partial view in place of a view of the whole. After all, some individuals who are very prominent and who identify themselves as Jews have been "excommunicated" by certain synagogal groups. So we are left with but one open possibility; to acknowledge the individual's right of decision. This seems to me to be the most satisfactory of all the alternatives, because it leaves all adventitious factors of birth and ancestry, training and nurture, out of the question, and identifies as Jews "them which say they are Jews."[11]

Now to ask whether there is any way in which the two previous aspects of this discussion can be related to each other seems no longer a valid question. Given the interpretation of "Jewry" that has just been presented, to say that the patterns of American culture and religion are reflected in American Jewry is almost to assert a triviality. For if Jewry is what those men and women of any time and place who say they are Jews believe and practice, then it follows that their beliefs and practices will inevitably reflect the cultural and religious conditions of the time and place in which they live. We can, I think, develop a formal statement that will express this relationship and be applicable to Jews living in America as well as to Jews living anywhere else in the world. This might be expressed in some such form as: There are, at all times and places where Jews reside, two chief constellations of forces operating to shape the spiritual life of the Jewish people; one of these is the aggregate of external forces working on the Jews from the host culture; the other is the aggregate of the internal forces of the varieties of Judaism brought by the Jewish group from its previous places of residence. The resultant of these two constellations of forces ultimately is a new variety of Judaism. On the basis of this formula we may take the fact of cultural reflection for granted and devote ourselves to seeing how the specific elements in American religious culture to which reference has been made—protestantism, pluralism, moralism, and voluntaryism—have been reflected in American-Jewish life.

Now, neither protestantism nor moralism is at all strange to Jewish life, and pluralism has appeared in Jewry occasionally, though it has not been a consistent element. In the sense in which the term "protestantism" is being used here—namely, the open acknowledgment that a variety of religious conclusions may be reached from identical or closely similar starting points—the Talmud itself bears evidence that multiplicity of opinions not only occurred but also was, if not joyously welcomed, at least tolerated, and that minority opinion was carefully preserved, just as it is in American Supreme Court practice. Furthermore, it is hard to point to any critical epoch in Jewish history in which sectarian divisions did not appear within Judaism as the institutional forms given to differing conclusions from the same data. More often than is apparent in the usual quick survey of Jewish history, these sectarian divisions hardened into denominations.

It would be easy, too, to demonstrate that Judaism has character-istically inclined to moralism rather than to ecclesiasticism, certainly since the destruction of the Second Temple, and possibly since the age of the Prophets. Every religious movement is the institutional-ization of a program. Where its emphasis remains predominantly on the program, it tends to be moralistic, but where its emphasis is markedly on the preservation of the institution itself, it tends to ecclesiasticism. Each of the living religions of the world has worked out its own balance of these two factors. Jewish stress has remained fixed for many centuries (sometimes, perhaps, with too great an attention to minutiae) on its program for living a good life. Institutional arrangements have been secondary to this purpose.

One great reason has been that, from the destruction of the Temple until quite recent days, there has been no important professional class whose income has been tied to institutionalized Judaism. With no clerical class, there has been no seduction to ecclesiasticism. Thus, protestantism and moralism have been perennial factors in Jewish life. As for pluralism, which, as used here, is the admission of the validity of a variety of starting points, to a certain extent it has been forced on the Jews by their status as a perpetual minority in dispersion. Judaism has long had to learn the lesson of living with other religions so that it is not surprising to find that the first philosophic defense of a radical religious pluralism was written by a dissident Jew, Baruch Spinoza. In addition to this general pluralistic bias, however, there have been certain periods in Jewish history, notably the Hellenistic age and the Golden Age of Spanish Jewry, when pluralistic multiplicity has been a major feature of Jewish religious life; and there have been other periods in which pluralism did not show itself to a significant degree.

The fact that Jewish life had manifested these traits in earlier epochs and in different lands meant that when, in the United States, a culture that supported these traits was host to Jewry, the traits themselves were exaggerated, possibly to the point of distortion. So, for example, as was suggested earlier, no overarching unity has developed in American Jewry, despite a number of attempts during the past century. Instead of unity, there has come about a ''protestantization'' of American Jewry into congregational bodies, each of which is to all intents and purposes completely independent of every other congregation, a law unto itself. By and large, these independent and autonomous congregations are member-controlled; that is to say, whatever authority the spiritual leader may have is the result of his personal influence over the voting members of his congregation and is not in any way consequent upon his ordination. These independent synagogues are loosely federated into denominations—Orthodox, Conservative, and Reform—but the denominational bodies have only the power to advise, not to enforce. The worst threat that a denominational group can make is that it will expel a member congregation; but this must be accounted as a greater threat to the denomination, which would lose both in numerical strength and in income by expelling the member congregation, than to the congregation itself, which would lose nothing except its right to be given the advice that it did not accept.

The denominational federations are, therefore, very weak, and policies are, in practice, determined by laymen at the congregational level. Since Jewish laymen spend only a fragment of their time with religious concerns, even as do laymen in most other religious groups, the decisions that are made are based more on the laymen's American experience than on their Jewish background. Furthermore, since the division between denominations is, in any case, rather subtle, requiring theological training to perceive its nuances, and since the laymen who determine practice are, for the most part, theologically naïve, it has become virtually impossible to detect any significant boundaries between Reform and Conservative congregational practice on the one side, Orthodox and Conservative on the other. The denominations shade off into one another. That there are three denominations seems to be accidental. There might just as well have been only two, or, for that matter, five or six or ten. Within each of the present three denominations there is a differentiation of factional groups that may, in time, lead to further fragmentation. There is even, to complete the analogy to Protestant Christianity, a nascent "ecumenical" movement in American Jewry, which, if it does not succeed in bringing about a broader-than-denominational unity of congregations, does at least bring together the rabbis who are officially attached to the various denominations within a certain geographical area. That this is the form of the American Jewish ecumenical movement is particularly interesting in view of the historical fact that the separation of the Orthodox and Conservative denominations came about because the founding fathers of American Orthodox Judaism refused to recognize the ordination of rabbinical graduates of the Jewish Theological Seminary.

In large measure, then, both the formation of denominations and the blurring of denominational lines is to be attributed to lay control of the synagogues in the United States. Lay control is not, however, a novelty in American Jewish life. It is a trait that has long been evident in European Jewry situations, especially among Jews of Sephardic background.[12] Lay control is also a feature of many

varieties of Protestant Christianity. The laws of many of the states in
the United States on the incorporation of religious groups are so
drawn as to encourage lay control. In addition, lay control suggests
the application of democratic practice in the realm of religious
organization. Again we find that a dominant tendency in American
life has reinforced a trait already present in Jewish life and produced,
as a consequence, an extreme and very tenacious strain in American
Jewry.

With regard to moralism, the situation closely parallels that of
"protestantism." Judaism has long inclined toward moralism.
Through most of Jewish history, however, this tendency has
expressed itself through the synagogue or its communal adjuncts. If
there was any group of the "unsynagogued," it was composed of
those who no longer regarded themselves as Jews. In American life,
where moralism has been extended to the point where it might
claim status as a denomination among other denominations (in the
form of Ethical Culture, for example) and where moralism has
infected even the most ecclesiastically oriented of the churches,
moralism among Jews has developed even farther. Many of the
unsynagogued—a group that begins to show itself in America in
the mid-eighteeth century[13]—regard themselves not merely as Jews,
but even as *good* Jews, and are so regarded by others as well,
because they devote themselves to "good causes." Some of these
causes are within Jewish life—Jewish hospitals, Jewish education,
Zionism or anti-Zionism, the defense against anti-Semitism, the
Jewish labor movement, and other such activities. For these, at least
a tenuous connection with Jewry can be found, and therefore at
least a minimal ethnic justification can be adduced for the Jewishness of the participant, even where support of the causes is
combined with forthright opposition to ritual and ceremonial law
and with constant attacks on the synagogues and their functionaries. But other "good Jews" of this moralistic variety may devote
their efforts to causes that have no direct involvement with Jewry in
any way whatsoever—scouting, or fresh air camps, or interracial
integration, or slum clearance, or aid for victims of multiple
sclerosis—all worthy causes, unquestionably, but without a shred of
specifically Jewish content. If any should be presumptuous enough
to ask why activities of this sort should prove the participant a Jew,

and a good Jew, too, the answer would be that the participant was "inspired" by Jewish ethical ideals in his loyal devotion to the cause. Presumably, too, the more prominent the individual concerned, the more likely that this defense would be offered and accepted.

Thus far, what we have discussed is the moralism of the unsynagogued. There is also a moralism of those who still retain membership in the synagogues but attend worship only on rare occasions, perhaps on the most important Holy Days or when there is a memorial service. Many of this type are nominally members of Orthodox synagogues—the "unobservant orthodox," they were called by Marshall Sklare.[14] As the synagogues have expanded their social programs, they have provided new outlets that may ultimately destroy their central religious function. For, after all, the man who has attended a Zionist meeting at his synagogue on Monday evening, a Men's Club meeting on Tuesday evening, an Anti-Defamation League meeting on Wednesday evening, and a meeting to plan a new gymnasium for the religious school on Thursday evening is likely to greet Friday evening with relief and to regard it as a heaven-sent opportunity to stay home and catch up on family affairs, and Saturday morning as a chance to wash the car and do other chores around the house and garden. Such a man has become, or remained, a synagogue member, but his true affiliation is with Jewish moralism, not Jewish religion.

For all that has been said, the key to understanding American Jewry as an emergent variety lies in the concept of voluntaryism. Of the four traits that have been mentioned, voluntaryism is the only novel factor, unknown in Jewish experience prior to Jewry's American sojourn, contributed by American culture to Jewish life. In respect to the other three traits, American culture was described as reinforcing an already existing trait of Jewry. Voluntaryism, or the idea that a man's religious affiliations are his own concern and not the business of the community, is now fairly common in Europe. This was not the case in the late eighteenth and early nineteenth centuries. Then voluntaryism was a novelty of the American scene. Even when the concept was accepted in certain parts of Europe, Western Europe was the first to be affected. Since the bulk of later Jewish immigration to the United States came from Eastern Europe, an environment of voluntaryism was a novelty to practically all Jews at the time of their arrival in America.

Essentially, what voluntaryism has meant to the individual Jew is that his civil status, whether as a citizen or as a wage earner, has been made independent of his Jewish ties. He has political rights because he is a man, not because he is a Jew. Officially, at least, his economic position is his by virtue of his common humanity and his unique abilities, rather than of his particular Jewishness. In some professions he still comes under a quota system; but it is not a governmental *numerus clausus*. Except in the form of "goals for affirmative action programs" the quota system has no official sanction and, in some instances, must be expressed by indirection in order to avoid official recrimination. In short, voluntaryism has proved to be the capstone of Jewish emancipation, for it has emancipated the Jews of America from any necessary connection with Jewry. If a Jew in America supports Judaism, he does so because it is his will to do so; if he does not support Judaism, his will is again his law. Pluralism, protestantism, and moralism are live religious options for the American Jew because voluntaryism has made him completely independent of synagogue control. That he has exercised his option of voluntaryism is indicated by the discrepancy between Jewish population and synagogue membership wherever in the United States accurate figures are available. Voluntaryism primarily, and secondarily the reemphasis on pluralism, protestantism, and moralism, are the forces shaping the American Jewish group into an American Jewry made in the reflection of American cultural and religious patterns.

Historical Sketch

How Judaism Came to North America

There is a persistent legend that Christopher Columbus was a member of a Spanish Jewish family. At the least, he is thought to have been the scion of a family of Spanish Marranos: forced converts to Christianity who maintained some measure of Jewish traditional practice as a private and secret family custom. These stories are probably merely fantasies—not, in the first instance, of Jews, for the Italian archbishop of Nebbio, Augustino Justiniani, who wrote an early account of Columbus and his discovery of the Americas, claimed to have known the family of Columbus in Genoa. There is no question, however, that the crew of Columbus' first voyage did include Jews. The ship's doctor was a Jew, Maestre Bernal. Possibly the first crew member actually to set foot on land was a Jew (or Marrano), Luis de Torres.[1]

This early participation of Jews in a dangerous voyage of exploration should surprise no one, for it merely extends the role that the Jews, of southern Europe especially, had played in the development of European trade. The date of this venture under the leadership of Columbus is, however, of importance, for in the year 1492 the Jews were expelled from Spain by edict of King Ferdinand and Queen Isabella. The expulsion, heralded by a record of persecutions during the fifteenth century, signaled the end of one of the finest periods of Jewish history, a truly Golden Age. The discovery of the Americas, leading to permanent European settlement, is the seed from which a new Golden Age of Jewry has developed in the United States.

The first Jewish settlers in the New World are found in the colonies of Spain and of Portugal (where a decree of expulsion had been issued in 1497). Years before the British had begun to establish colonies on the North American continent, there were Jews of Iberian background living on the Caribbean islands and in the Portuguese colony of Brazil. Some of these early settlers were Marranos who seized the opportunity afforded by remoteness from the home country and from church authorities to return openly to the practice of Judaism. The first synagogues to be formed in the New World, the earliest Jewish cemeteries on American soil, even the first tentative ventures in Jewish education, all were instituted by Spanish and Portuguese Jews, *Sephardim* (*Sepharad* is the Hebrew name for Spain and, by extension, all of Iberia).

When the Dutch, in the mid-seventeenth century, challenged Portuguese sovereignty in Brazil, some of the Brazilian Jews joined with the attacking forces, while others, apparently, served the Dutch cause as secret agents. Why they did so is easily understood, for at this time Holland, of all the nations of Europe, was by far the most tolerant of religious diversity. When the Portuguese succeeded in meeting and defeating the Dutch challenge, however, those Jews who had cast their lot with the Dutch had to move again. One small group of twenty-three, in 1654, arrived in the Dutch colony of New Amsterdam on the French ship *Sainte Catherine,* the Jewish *Mayflower.*

The authorities of New Amsterdam were not eager to extend the hospitality of their small settlement on the tip of Manhattan Island to these wandering Jews. The Jews, for example, had to struggle for the right to share guard duties with other settlers. We may understand this struggle as the attempt of the new arrivals to establish their status as residents of the settlement and to indicate to the authorities their readiness to share the burdens of the community, in confrontation with a resolve of the authorities that the Jews were merely visitors, tolerated for a time.

In any case, the Jews of New Amsterdam, like other residents who were not Dutch, were not permitted to establish a public house of worship. There are no synagogue records preserved of earlier date than 1728, by which time New Amsterdam had become New York, and British authorities had superseded the Dutch. We can only guess at the early religious life of these first Jews in North America. They probably worshiped in private homes from the very beginning of their life in New Amsterdam. (A *minyan*—ten adult males—is the only requirement for the holding of Jewish worship services). Public services may have been held as early as 1673 and were certainly held by 1682. The first synagogue building of which we have record was the Mill Street Synagogue, built in 1729, but an earlier map of New York, drawn by John Miller in 1695, shows the site of a "Jews' synagogue" on Beaver Street. The official religious life of the group began much earlier, however, not long after their arrival, when in 1656 permission was reluctantly granted the Jews of New Amsterdam to purchase land for a cemetery.[2]

Permission to acquire this burial ground must have been given (14 July 1656) very soon after Governor Peter Stuyvesant had received a letter (dated 13 March 1656) from the directors of the Dutch West India Company in Amsterdam, repeating earlier instructions that the Jews in New Amsterdam were to have the same privileges as those in Amsterdam, but "only as far as civil and political rights are concerned, without giving the said Jews a claim to the privilege of exercising their religion in a synagogue or a [public] gathering." There could scarcely have been time, by 14 July, in that age of slower communications, for Stuyvesant to have received the directors' letter of 14 June 1656, spelling out the limited measure of religious toleration to be extended to the Jews, who "shall not be employed in any public service . . . nor allowed to have open retail shops; but they may quietly and peacefully carry on their business as beforesaid and exercise in all quietness their religion within their houses, for which end they must without doubt endeavor to build their houses, close together in a convenient place on one or the other side of New Amsterdam—at their choice—as they do here [in Amsterdam]."[3] Thus the directors suggested that the commercial expertness of the Jews, especially in the wholesale trade, was to be fostered, as it was in the home country, but that the right of public worship was not to be granted. At this time, the beautiful synagogue in Amsterdam was flourishing. We should note, moreover, that in this letter the directors made the assumption that the Jews would live in close proximity to each other, on their own volition, but under the inner compulsion of religious need. The directors, then, expected that a voluntary ghetto would develop in New Amsterdam.

The Colonial Period

When the British captured New Amsterdam and renamed it New York, they confirmed the rights and privileges allowed its citizens by the Dutch authorities. This was all the more necessary because, as a colony chartered by the Crown, New York had an established church, the Church of England. Now even the well-to-do Dutch burghers were members of a dissenting religious group. They were sufficiently prominent to be able to demand toleration of their own church. In a society where the established church was forced to extend toleration to another church, toleration for Jews was all but automatic. During the years of British rule, the small Jewish group in New York City, formally organized under the name of Shearith Israel (Remnant of Israel), carried on services, except for a period during the Revolution itself when many of its members whose sympathies were with the fighters for independence retired to Philadelphia and merged their worship with that of the Phila-delphia synagogue.

In addition, the officers of Shearith Israel managed the cemetery. Members as well as officers participated in subordinate mutual aid societies that enabled them to fulfill religious commandments (*mitzvot*), by assisting in preparing the dead for burial or giving help to the bereaved family. Shearith Israel also provided, in connection with its Mill Street Synagogue, a ritual bath (*mikvah*) where the women of the congregation might perform their religious purifications at appropriate times. The congregational minute-books show that the officers were concerned with the supervision of the ritual slaughterer (*shochet*), to make sure that he performed his functions properly and to assure themselves that the meat sold to Jews was prepared according to the traditional regulations (*kosher*). At this period, indeed, the slaughterer was an employee of Shearith Israel. In a similar fashion, the synagogue assumed responsibility for assuring an adequate supply of correctly prepared unleavened bread (*matzot*) for the Passover holiday. The Board, through a committee, negotiated a fair price with the baker, examined his ovens to be sure that they fulfilled the requirements, and super-vised the actual baking process as a further guarantee of propriety. One of the major responsibilities of Shearith Israel at this time was to carry on the education of the Jewish children of the city. At least as early as 1755, and perhaps earlier, in the absence of alternative arrangements for the "secular" education of Jewish children, the congregational school taught Spanish, English com-position, and arithmetic as well as religious subjects. It is worthy of note, especially in the light of the general neglect of the education of girls in traditional Jewish circles, that the Shearith Israel congregational school was coeducational by 1790. Generally the reader (*hazzan*) of the Congregation carried on the duties of the teacher in the school, with additional compensation for his extra work.

Similar patterns for synagogue activity, differing only in minor detail from those of Shearith Israel, are to be found in the early histories of the other pre-Revolutionary Jewish synagogues in the British colonies. In Newport, Rhode Island, Jews settled in 1658. The very tolerant rules of the Rhode Island colony under Roger Williams permitted the early establishment of a synagogue, Yeshuat Israel (Salvation of Israel), now called the Touro Synagogue in honor of a nineteenth-century benefactor. In the eighteenth cen-tury, however, Rhode Island fell away from its tolerant beginnings, and the Jewish community of Newport began to fade. The almost total eclipse of Newport's shipping during the Revolution and its failure to recover after the Peace of Ghent led to the abandonment of the city by the few Jewish merchants who had not left earlier, and thus the Newport synagogue became an empty ruin until it was revived as a showplace by Judah Touro's bequest. Other early synagogues were Mikveh Israel (Hope of Israel), Philadelphia, founded about 1745; Beth Elohim (House of God), Charleston, South Carolina, founded in 1750; and Mickve Israel (Hope of Israel), Savannah, Georgia, which may have been founded as early as 1733.[4]

It is noteworthy that all of these early synagogues in the British North American colonies were located in major seaports. Although many Jews of the colonial age may have engaged in other ways of making a living, international trade was still one of their important roles in the economy. It is also notable that there was no synagogue in the chief port city of the period, Boston, where a "native" merchant class had developed in the seventeenth century and where, therefore, there was no need for the special expertness in this middle-class occupation that the Jews had developed in the course of their European experience.[5]

All the synagogues that have been mentioned here were established according to the customary pattern of the Sephardim (*minhag sepharad*). The differences between this pattern and that followed by the Jews of Central and Eastern Europe (*Ashkenazim; minhag ashkenaz*) might seem minimal to the outsider. To the Jew himself, however, the inclusion or exclusion of a particular hymn, the use of one or another traditional chant, or the variant pronunciation of one of the sounds of Hebrew could never be trivial. Indeed, the less he knew of the basic meaning of Judaism and the less he had thought about its religious and ethical ideals, the more his religion was a matter of rote repetition and the more disturbed he could become at any departure from the pattern that he had learned. Neither the original Sephardic settlers nor the Ashkenazim from Germany, Holland, and England who followed in the eighteenth century and who soon (perhaps by 1730) outnumbered the earlier arrivals, were men of religious thought or learning. They were rather the more adventurous spirits, those who had the physical courage and the stamina to break away from their European roots and to risk life itself in a land that was all frontier.

The remarkable thing is that the numerically predominant Ashkenazim did not break with the religiously dominant Sephardic ritual. Perhaps they accommodated themselves because of the more settled status of the earlier arrivals. Had the order of arrival been reversed, it is probable that the Sephardim would have accepted an existing Ashkenazic *minhag*. The Jewish population was not large enough in colonial days, in any of the cities, to support two synagogues, two cemeteries, two ritual baths, two slaughterers, two teachers, two readers. So the Ashkenazim joined the Sephardic synagogues, sometimes married into Sephardic families, were elected to office in the synagogue, and learned to tolerate and in some cases to love the strange sound of the Sephardic *minhag*.

After the American Revolution

The handful of Jews in the United States were as divided in opinion on the Revolution as were the non-Jews. Of those who supported the Revolutionary cause, some participated actively in military affairs. The records of the pension office of the United States show several Jews who served in the Continental Army. Others helped to furnish supplies for the army.[6] Probably the best known figure was Haym Salomon, whose small fortune was placed at the disposal of the revolutionary government. The amount of money involved was trivial, and Salomon's action was important mainly because it symbolized the fact that a number of Jews already considered themselves American to the core.[7] During the long years of the Revolution, the synagogues, except for Shearith Israel, continued to function, modified the special prayers for the government, and joined with the Christian churches of the land in observing the fast days and days of solemn assembly proclaimed by the civil and military authorities.

When the war had ended, Jews began to enter the service of the new government in a variety of roles. Although, by our later standards, the American Jews of that age were barely literate, their level of literacy was higher than that of the general population, so that they could be immediately useful in government service.[8] Because the United States was a new country and because the traditions of exclusion that were firmly rooted in European life had not gained a foothold in the colonial world, there was a remarkable absence of prejudice against the Jews. The freedom of religion that soon became national policy and was all but universal in the state governments was surely not introduced as a matter of justice to the Jews or to Judaism. Yet the Jews were among its beneficiaries, both individually, in that their religion was no barrier to their entry into any career, and collectively, in that the open practice of Judaism was at no time threatened by governmental action.

In 1783, when the American Revolution was barely finished, the enlightened Jewish literary idol of the Berlin salons, Moses Mendelssohn, wrote a short treatise advocating religious freedom and the separation of church and state. How meaningful the geographically

remote American experience was to him is indicated by a foot-
note added to the last page of the first edition of his *Jerusalem:*
"Alas! We hear from America that the [Continental] Congress has
revived the old tune and is beginning to talk of a dominant
religion."[9] From time to time in American history, talk of this sort
has recurred. Amendments to the Constitution of the United States
declaring it to be a "Christian nation" have been proposed, but
never adopted. Anti-Jewish sentiment among the American people
has waxed and waned, but there has never been an official
governmental policy of restricting either the opportunities open to
individual Jews or the freedom of Jewish worship.

There were such restrictions in most of the countries of Europe,
and especially in the German states during the first half of the
nineteenth century. Consequently, to emigrate to the United States
was the dream of many Jews, particularly from those states, like
Hesse and Cassell, in which the restrictions placed on Jews were
most oppressive.[10] From these central European states, from Holland, and from England came the Jewish immigrants before the
Civil War. Though they were still the more daring members of their
European communities, they were more highly educated than those
who had preceded them and, in particular, were more conversant
with the Jewish tradition. Soon after this newer group of immigrants arrived on the American scene, they began to establish
synagogues of their own, following the ritual pattern to which they
had been accustomed in their places of origin. Thus the second,
larger group of synagogues founded in the United States followed
the Ashkenazic *minhag,* in its German form.

Hebrew, though differently pronounced, was, of course, the
sacred language of the new arrivals, but whereas the secondary,
semi-sacred language of the Sephardic synagogues had been Spanish, that of the later synagogues was German. The minute-books of
these congregations were kept in German (or in Judeo-German, the
"classic" form of Yiddish); such occasional preaching as was
ventured by the readers (*hazzanim*) in their synagogues—for they
had, as yet, no rabbis—was in German; their prayers, when
translated at all, were translated into German. Although they
soon began to use English as their medium of secular communication, the use of German as the secondary language of the
synagogue persisted for some time.

The wave of German-Jewish immigration spread out more widely in the United States than the earlier Sephardic ripple, in part because urban centers away from the Atlantic coast had begun to develop by the time these immigrants arrived. Soon there were Ashkenazic synagogues in cities like Albany, Pittsburgh, and Cincinnati. After the Louisiana Purchase had added the vast drainage basin of the Mississippi River system to the United States, synagogues appeared in the cities of this region, like St. Louis and New Orleans. There was no significant movement of Jews into rural areas. The habit of centuries of forced urbanization of the Jews in Europe persisted even when there were no laws forbidding the Jews to own land. But as new urban centers developed in the westward spread of the American people, Jewish families were among the early inhabitants and synagogues were founded soon thereafter.

Not all of the Ashkenazic migrants came from Germany. Some had lived in England, others in Holland, and still others in those parts of Poland that had been assigned to Germany in the still-recent partition of Poland in 1793. Where the Jewish population of an American city was large enough to sustain several small synagogues, these tended to follow the special traditions of the various countries from which the immigrants had come. In New York City, for example, the first Ashkenazic break with Shearith Israel did not come until 1825, when there were about three hundred Jews in the city. Before this date, the group may, however, have conducted services according to the Ashkenazic *minhag* in a special *minyan* under the auspices of Shearith Israel. This was the expedient used in Philadelphia for a number of years. In New York the leaders of the Ashkenazic secession were of English descent. They founded Congregation B'nai Jeshurun as the Ashkenazic house of worship. Not long afterward, in 1828, many of the German, Dutch, and Polish Jews in the membership of B'nai Jeshurun seceded and formed their own congregation, Anshe Chesed. A decade later, when the number of New York Jews of Polish descent had increased, the Polish Jews in Anshe Chesed banded together with those who had remained in B'nai Jeshurun and with the more recently arrived Polish Jews to form a congregation that followed the Polish variety of general Ashkenazic practice. They gave the name of Shaarey Zedek to this new synagogue. Because there was less Jewish emigration from Holland, it was not until 1847 that there were enough Dutch Jews to support a synagogue, which was called B'nai Israel.

In all the instances that have been mentioned, the grounds of secession were, in an extended sense, religious. There was, it is true, basic agreement upon the fundamentals of the faith. These were not schismatic, heretical groups, nor did they herald a "Reform" movement. All followed the rabbinic interpretation of biblical law as codified in the *Shulhan Arukh* of Joseph Caro, supplemented, in the case of all the Ashkenazic groups, by the annotations of Moses Isserles. The major sections of the worship service remained as they had been fixed by the ancient rabbis perhaps as early as the first century of the common era. All maintained the age-old messianic hope of a time when the scattered remnants of the children of Israel would be led in a triumphal return to the Holy Land by a divinely ordained Messiah, born of the Davidic line. They were one in faith, one in law, one in hope—and yet they felt more at ease spiritually when worshiping with those whose customs of dress, of food, of dialect were their own.

This was, needless to say, a period during which the Jewish population of New York was growing rapidly, so that by the middle of the nineteenth century it was by far the largest aggregation of Jews in the United States. Where there were fewer Jews, fragmentation could not occur to the same extent, for even if we discount the practical question of meeting a budget, we must not overlook the requirement that public worship include a minimum of ten adult males. Many a smaller Jewish community in the United States could barely muster a *minyan*. Accommodation to one another, even compromise on profoundly meaningful customs of the "home" country, had to be the order of the day. Philadelphia Jewry and New York Jewry could afford the luxury of schism and secession; the Jews of Norfolk could not.

Even in New York and Philadelphia there were those who saw that the chaos of disunity was undesirable and inefficient. Advocates of unity realized, however, that no compulsory union could be enforced, either on a local or on a national basis. The suggested plans were, therefore, of a voluntary nature. Most followed the common understanding of the pattern of the federal government and of many Protestant bodies in the United States in proposing plans for federation rather than amalgamation. Proponents of these plans thought that independent congregations might be willing to join together for a particular purpose without giving up their autonomy in any other respect. Thus, three German-Jewish synagogues in New York City, Anshe Chesed, Rodeph Shalom, and Shaarey Hashamayim, mutually agreed, in 1845, to hire Dr. Max Lilienthal, who had then recently come to New York, as their rabbi and director of the religious school of the three congregations. Anshe Chesed backed out because the proposal involved a merger of the religious schools. In 1847, Anshe Chesed was ready to join again, but by this time the move for a German-Jewish community had lost its vitality, and the united religious school dissolved along with the communal union.[11]

Among the earliest and most dedicated advocates of some measure of religious unity the Reverend Isaac Leeser of Congregation Mikveh Israel of Philadelphia deserves special mention. Leeser, who became reader of Mikveh Israel as a young man in 1829, was a relatively well-educated literary figure and scholar, although he had no rabbinic ordination. As early as 1830, Leeser began regularly to preach in English at the Sabbath services. He seems to have recognized the need for a conscious and carefully selective inclusion of American cultural elements into Jewish life, lest the unconscious, unthinking, unselective acceptance of American ways should go too far. *The Occident and American Jewish Advocate*, the journal Leeser inaugurated in 1843, had a strongly traditionalist orientation. By the issue of January 1844, Leeser's editorial, entitled "The Demands of the Times," called for unity of religious observance under a universally accepted religious law. Although he asserted that he favored "municipal autonomy of each separate synagogue," he urged the development of a feeling of unity and community, if not actual union. Returning to the same theme, under the same title, a month later, Leeser demanded "a *federative* union," to be formed in spite of the "many inveterate prejudices among our people" which, he thought at this time, had no religious basis but rested on differences in wealth, nationality, and degree of concern for reform.

Even before *The Occident* had been founded, Leeser and his Philadelphia colleague, Louis Salomon, reader of the Ashkenazic

Congregation Rodeph Shalom, had drawn up a plan for a federation of synagogues. This proposal for union was broached by Leeser
and Salomon in 1841. In 1845 an elaboration of the original
proposal, now incorporating suggestions from leaders of Beth
Israel, Philadelphia's third synagogue, was published in *The
Occident* together with a call for a national congress to make the
synagogal union a reality. The synagogues of the country were not
ready for such an action, however. Far more representative of the
thinking of members and leaders throughout the country is the
following resolution, adopted by Congregation Beth Elohim of
Charleston, South Carolina, 10 August 1841: "Resolved that all
conventions, founded or created for the establishment of any
ecclesiastical authority whatever, ... are alien to the spirit and
genius of the age in which we live, and are wholly inconsistent with
the spirit of American Liberty."[12] Almost every group asserted its
right to remain independent of any form of centralized control.
Henry S. Morais's comment on the pluralism of Philadelphia Jewry
serves as an apt characterization of Jewish synagogue organization
throughout the United States in mid-nineteenth century: "No
ecclesiastical authority existing [among the Jews] in this country,
matters were allowed to shape their own course—each Congregation doing as it saw fit, without referring its action to any but its
own minister, and even he, at times, was overruled by the laymen
who composed the membership of the Board of Trustees."[13] While
such a mood prevailed, the Philadelphia plan for religious union
was bound to be rejected out of hand.

Stirrings of Reform

The chief support for Isaac Leeser's demand for a union of
congregations came from Rabbi Isaac Mayer Wise. Wise, who has
been called the "master architect of Reform religious institutions,"[14] was certainly not motivated by the same regard for
traditionalism that moved Leeser. Nevertheless, he felt as keenly as
Leeser that the anarchic development of the American synagogues
created an unfortunate situation in American Judaism. Unlike
other rabbis of Central European origin, Wise believed with Leeser
that conscious adaptation of Judaism to the American scene was

both necessary and desirable. He went so far as to propose that a distinctive American version of the traditional liturgy and ritual was called for. When he published a prayer book for his own Reform congregation in Cincinnati, he titled it *Minhag Amerika*. In 1848 Wise prepared for publication in *The Occident* a call "To the Ministers & Other Israelites" for a grand association of "Israelitish" congregations in North America.[15]

Wise argued for national Jewish union on utilitarian grounds, but it was *religious* rather than *practical* utility that was his chief concern. "Now in order to fulfil our sacred mission, to send our important message to mankind, it behooves us to be united as one man; to be linked together by the ties of equal views concerning religious questions—by uniformity in our sacred customs, in our forms of worship, and religious education. We ought to have a uniform system for our schools, Synagogues, benevolent societies— for all our religious institutions." The seeds of disagreement were already clearly present, even in this brief statement, for the notion of a Jewish mission among the nations, as a substitute for the messianic hope of a restored Jewish nation, was one of the hallmarks of the nascent Reform movement in German Jewry. Since Leeser was insistent upon the literal teaching of the doctrine of the coming of the Messiah, his view and Wise's were impossible of ultimate reconciliation or compromise.

Wise continued his "call" by commenting, most revealingly, on the founding and current leadership of American Jewry. He asserted that the majority of American Jewish congregations "are generally composed of the most negative elements from all the different parts of Europe and elsewhere; they have been founded and are now governed for the greater part by men of no considerable knowledge of our religion, and generally of no particular zeal for our common cause. The consequence of all this is, that many congregations have no solid basis, no particular stimulus to urge on the youth to a religious life, and no nourishment for the spiritual Israelite." Concluding his remarks, Wise indicated explicitly his feeling that the unity for which he was pleading should follow the lines of a moderate reform. He called especially for the German rabbis in the country, those who had been directly exposed to the beginnings of European Reform Judaism, to join him in his plea for concerted action by the Jewish congregations in the United States. Leeser commented editorially on Wise's "call," saying that he endorsed the idea of meeting but did not agree with all of Wise's views. He tied his sense of the need for meeting to the revolutionary events that were then (1848) taking place all over Europe. The tone of Leeser's statement is marked by a mild turning from the notion of Jewish emancipation to the reaffirmation of the doctrine of Israel's election: "In the present whirl of passions which have been let loose over the world, the Jews are running the danger of losing themselves in the agitation of public affairs, and forgetting that they are men who have other duties to perform, besides voting at elections, and fighting in battles.... The present actual or approaching freedom of mingling as a Jew with the masses, does not of right empower him to cast away his privilege of being one of God's chosen people."[16] Again, in May 1849, under the title "Shall We Meet?" Leeser editorially endorsed the idea of a meeting of all American Jewish congregations. In this editorial, however, he specifically rejected the view that a general reform of religious practices should be one objective of the meeting: "We should regard a general reform by the authority of a convention as the greatest evil which could by possibility befall our people. In using the word reform, we employ it in the sense which it usually bears in the present age,—*a violent change and a substitution of new notions in the place of well-established customs and opinions.* ... But there is another reform, which looks to the removal of municipal abuses, as we may term them; ... we see no reason why German [Ashkenazic] and Portuguese [Sephardic] Jews could not unite in one common effort to establish a better state of things, without yielding in the least their peculiarities, or their independence."[17] The lines on which the battle would have developed are clear; Leeser wanted a national convention of American congregations in order to block the Reform impulse, while Wise wanted a national convention in order to create an authority to sanction a moderate Reform program. The proposed meeting was never held, however.

It is nevertheless fruitful to consider the movement toward Reform that lies behind the story of the national meeting that never occurred. Much of the background cannot be told here in detail, for it is part of the history of Judaism in Western Europe. Gradually, over the three centuries between the expulsion of the Jews from Spain and Portugal and the French Revolution, while the Jews of Eastern Europe were developing a rich and full culture based almost exclusively upon Jewish sources, the Jews of Western Europe were coming increasingly in contact with the non-Jewish culture of the surrounding world. As individuals, the Jews benefited from the developing individualism that followed on the breakdown of the feudal order in the West. As a group, Jews gained a certain amount of security from the enlarged theory of toleration of religious differences that flowed, in large measure, from the Protestant Reformation. More and more, Jews found ways of acquiring a secular education to supplement their religious training, and, partially as a consequence, came to an appreciation of some of the aesthetic ideals of Western Europe.

From these intellectual and aesthetic perspectives, some Central European Jews began to take a closer look at the traditional customs and practices of Judaism, and they did not altogether like what they saw. Through the Middle Ages and, in Eastern Europe, into modern times, Jews had been able to compare their own culture favorably with what they saw around them. Now, for the first time, some of them felt that it was Jewish culture that lacked finesse, that was barbaric and crude. An oft-repeated criticism indicted Judaism for its perpetuation of "Oriental" elements. Compared with the brief worship services of the Protestant churches, Jewish services were long and the behavior of the worshipers was indecorous. Compared with the rich liturgical symbolism of the Roman Catholic services, Jewish services were pallid, colorless. For the man who had absorbed the cultural values of Western societies in the glorious age of baroque church music, the lack of instrumental music and the traditional forms of cantillation used by the reader in Jewish services signified aesthetic barbarism. The early stirrings of the Reform impulse in Holland in 1796, in Germany after 1817, and in the United States (in Charleston, South Carolina) in 1824, centered in a demand that the ritual of the synagogue should be purged of the accretions of the centuries and restored to its classical simplicity and brevity so that Jewish services might achieve the intelligibility, dignity, and decorum of Protestant worship.[18] In a burst of fine rhetoric, they

said: "We wish not to *overthrow*, but to *rebuild*; we wish not to
destroy, but to *reform* and *revise* the evils complained of; we wish
not to *abandon* the institutions of Moses, but to *understand and
observe them*; in fine we wish to worship God, not as *slaves of
bigotry and priestcraft*, but as the enlightened descendants of that
chosen race."[19] The earnest advocates of these changes did not
suspect how quickly devoutness can fly out the window when
decorum walks in at the door.

Later a need was felt for philosophical and theological justification of these ritual modifications. In German Reform Judaism
this need was met in two ways. First, beginning in 1819, a group of
young men began to study Judaism critically and objectively, yet
with sympathy, on the model of studies carried on in the universities. These scholars, working under the banner of "academic
study of Judaism" (*Wissenschaft des Judenthums*), explored the
history of Judaism, its literature, its cultural monuments, and its
social matrix in different eras. The methods they employed were
those of the academic disciplines, for the first time consistently
applied to investigations of Judaism. Not all of these scholars had
Reform proclivities, but the combined impact of their various
studies bolstered the Reform movement by demonstrating that
changes such as the Reformers proposed were not historically
unprecedented. They showed that literary and religious creativity
had been perennially alive in Judaism, so that this ancient religion
had continued through the ages to produce new ideas and new
patterns of expression appropriate to the time and place of their
development. In the absence of either rabbinical or qualified
general scholarship among the Jews of America before 1850, there
was no American parallel to this German-Jewish group, but its
influence was felt after 1850.

In the second place, modifications and innovations in Judaism
have traditionally been made by the authority of rabbis acting in
concert, as in a synod or in the accepted legal precedents of a
rabbinical court. When, from time to time, it was necessary for a
single rabbi to enunciate a novel regulation, his act had only local
force unless and until it was validated by acceptance by a larger
group. Aware that this was the traditional and required mode of
change, the German Reform rabbis in Europe held conferences in

1844, 1845, and 1846, in the course of which they formulated and focused the principles of Reform Judaism. Nothing of this sort was possible in the United States before 1858 because there were virtually no ordained rabbis in the country. The spiritual leaders—however dedicated and respected they might be, like Isaac Leeser and, before him, Gershom Mendes Seixas, minister of Shearith Israel during and after the Revolution—were readers, who lacked the power to speak with authority on legal matters. In the 1840s a few ordained rabbis (and some others who claimed ordination but whose claim was never validated) came to America. Most of them had already committed themselves to at least a moderate program of Reform, but their congregants had not begun to think in these terms.

When Leeser and his associates in Philadelphia proposed a nationwide convention of synagogues—not a rabbinical conference—they were well aware that such a convention could recommend only the most superficial of changes. An English sermon might be introduced without rabbinical sanction; rules to produce more decorous behavior during the services might be promulgated without rabbinical sanction; but major changes required rabbis to authorize them, and most of the small number of rabbis in the United States were ready to go too far for Leeser's liking.

Leeser, too, declared that he wanted "improvements," but also expressed his "desire that nothing should be done hastily, or contrary to law." His reasons for seeking improvements were no different from those given by the advocates of Reform, "to bring the backsliders and the lukewarm back to the pale of religion."[20] He praised the leaders of English Jewry for cutting the length of the services, asserting that this would restore order and decorum. He went so far as to call it the "duty" of directors of synagogues to do whatever was necessary to produce improved order during worship. But in 1856 Leeser was faced with the charge, leveled at him by Rabbi Max Lilienthal (holder of a doctorate from the University of Munich and of impeccable ordination by Rabbi Hirsch Aub of Munich), that "it is the sincere wish of the editor of *The Occident,* that all should remain in *statu quo;* that a synod should be convened to declare innovation unlawful, and to sanction the *status quo* by their vote."[21] To this *ad hominem* and somewhat unfair attack, Leeser replied that reform of the ritual and services was proper, but that only ordained rabbis could legitimately reinterpret Jewish law. Even ordained rabbis, he continued, must be able to show that the changes they propose are not merely responses to the spirit of the age but are, rather, "decrees of the Most High." With this argument Leeser attempted to protect his form of traditionalism against the numerical preponderance of Reform rabbis.

Samuel Isaacs, editor of the *Jewish Messenger* and minister of Shaarey Tefillah in New York, seconded Leeser's efforts and echoed Leeser's themes when he wrote, "We want *reform*, not in the service, but within ourselves." This statement came toward the end of an editorial that began by calling attention to the need for more decorum during synagogue services. "It really appears to us that many of our co-religionists imagine God's house to be a place to see and be seen, to exhibit the last fashions, to listen to the news of the day, and to traduce the character of their neighbors.... Far better to remain in our own dwellings than to be an attendant at the house devoted to religion and to tarnish its purity by our earth-begotten ideas."[22] It may well be that the concern of traditionalists like Isaacs and Leeser for greater decorum during services was a response to the fact that in the United States, with its far more open social life, non-Jewish visitors were quite likely to be in attendance at the services of the synagogues. This was certainly the case at special services. Where there are records of the proceedings of dedicatory exercises for new synagogue buildings, the number and the distinction of non-Jewish participants is amazing. Even on ordinary occasions, there was much more intervisitation than had been the pattern in Europe. Jews were no less a curiosity in the United States; but it was important to their sense of belonging not to be an oddity.

Early Successes of Reform Judaism

The traditionalism with modest concessions to American manners that Leeser and Isaacs advocated was a last-ditch stand. It soon became evident that the Jews of the United States were moving toward the moderate Reform position of Isaac M. Wise, or even to the more extreme position of David Einhorn. By 1860, most of the descendants of the seventeenth- and eighteenth-century immigrants had been absorbed into America's Protestant majority by the process of intermarriage. The Reform tinge that was overwhelmingly preponderant in the thinking of the German-trained rabbis gradually entered the consciousness of their German-speaking congregants who constituted, at this time, the bulk of American Jewry. After 1848, especially, a small number of immigrants were of the middle class; a very few were men who had committed themselves irrevocably to the revolution of 1848, and who were therefore in an awkward position in Germany when the revolution failed.[23] Some members of this group were men of secular education and organizational skill. Under their impact practical reforms were introduced into older synagogues or new synagogues of Reform character were established in New York City, Baltimore, Albany, Cincinnati, Philadelphia, Chicago, and many smaller communities.

In addition, a distinctive Reform theory began to emerge. It involved considerable deemphasis of the ceremonial and ritual law, and hence a reduction of the significance of the Pentateuch and the classical rabbinical commentaries, and a corresponding increase in the attention given to the moral law and the prophetic books of the Old Testament. American Reform Judaism at this time followed closely its German source by minimizing the doctrine of the Chosen People and attempting to eliminate the residual nationalism of the messianic doctrine. The tension in traditional Judaism between its elements of universalism and particularism was replaced by an emphatic and explicit stress on prophetic universalism; but particularism was covertly reintroduced by the assertion of a special mission for the Jews among the nations. By accepting the evolutionary ideas that were prevalent in the intellectual world of the later nineteenth century, the spokesmen of Reform Judaism were able to maintain that their position represented the progressive element in the evolution of Judaism.[24] Thus, for example, Rabbi Joseph Krauskopf lectured on "Evolution and Judaism" at his synagogue in Kansas City, Missouri, in the winter of 1886–87.[25] Here he argued that "the mind has its eternal rights. When it has outlived an age it will not permit itself to be lulled to sleep by the lullabies of the past."[26]

The religion of Judaism, said Krauskopf, has gradually, over the centuries since Abraham, been purged of some of its grosser elements while other crude notions picked up by Judaism in its historical development still remain as a blot on the religion. "Beliefs and ceremonies and rites of the Acadians [sic] and of the Egyptians, of the Assyrians and Persians, of the Greeks and Romans, of Christian and Mohammedan borrowed heathenism, all these had sent their quota into the *Talmud,* into the *Caballah,* into the *Schulchan Aruch,* into the Ghetto synagogue, and this fantastic make-up received the name of Orthodox Judaism."[27] To this conception of Judaism, Krauskopf offered an alternative he called "the Judaism of to-day," the evolved form of Judaism. This is "purely a religion," purged of nationalistic elements. Its purpose is that of "acquainting us with that much of the nature of God, which is conceivable to the finite mind" and of indicating "the course we must pursue to live in the fullest harmony with the divine purpose for which we exist." Judaism is a morality and a historical continuity which "nevertheless strives to be in accord with the postulates of reason." Krauskopf's Reform Judaism cast into the discard the concept of a chosen people, a kingdom of priests and a holy nation. He referred to this doctrine as "that peculiarly Oriental notion." Judaism, he said, recognizes "the existence of religious evolution. . . . It takes cognizance of the spirit of the age. It retains such Biblical and rabbinical beliefs and ceremonies and institutions as tend to elevate and sanctify our lives, and rejects all such, which however comforting and useful they may have been in their day, have become obsolete, misleading, unsuited to the spiritual wants of the age."[28] Krauskopf was clearly disingenuous in asserting that he entered into his subject without preconceptions. He chose to discuss evolution because he saw in it a useful approach to the defense of Reform Judaism. By extending the scope of the theory of evolution from the biological to the religious understanding, he was able to translate the religious changes desired by Reform Judaism into the inevitable progress of religious evolution.

Joseph Krauskopf was one of the four young men who were ordained as rabbis in the first such ceremony to take place under the auspices of an American-Jewish institution. They were the first rabbis whose training was entirely American, the earliest members of a group that viewed Judaism in the United States out of an American background. The seminary that gave them their training was the Hebrew Union College in Cincinnati, founded, in 1875, by Isaac M. Wise and supported by the Union of American Hebrew Congregations, the voluntary organization of Reform congregations. Advocacy of a school for higher Jewish studies had been a recurrent feature of the editorials in both Isaac Leeser's *Occident* and Samuel Isaacs' *Jewish Messenger*. So, in the January 1847 issue of *The Occident*, Leeser called for the education of English-speaking scholars for the Jewish ministry. He argued that a school should be established, "whether in England or America, whence may issue men of ample religious and literary endowments, known to the congregations, and therefore likely to be chosen with a full knowledge of their personal history, in addition to that of their acquirements." The hint implicit in the latter part of this quotation was made explicit later in the editorial, when Leeser reproved the practice of importing German scholars whose personal background was unknown—and whose sympathies, not incidentally, were with Reform. Isaacs, in the *Jewish Messenger*, called for the foundation of a "Jews College of America."

Meantime, as early as 1854, Wise had announced a plan (in Robert Lyon's weekly, *The Asmonean*) for a Zion Collegiate Institute. A start toward fund raising was made, but the project did not mature. Again, in Baltimore, a group of young men representing an association of Hebrew literary societies called for the establishment of a National Hebrew College. In 1866, Benjamin Peixotto, then the Grand Master of the Independent Order of B'nai B'rith, tried unsuccessfully to finance an American Jewish university by voluntary contributions from the members of his order. In 1867 Leeser and a group of lay and ministerial coworkers founded Maimonides College in Philadelphia; it closed for lack of support in 1873. The Hebrew Union College, after many difficulties and much struggle, succeeded where all these prior suggestions and attempts had failed, and thus added to the prestige and increased the prominence of Reform Judaism.

Isaac Wise, with his constant commitment to organization for common purposes and with the example of the German Reform conferences to bolster his conviction that united action brought results, had organized small rabbinical conferences as early as 1855. By 1885, however, the Reform impulse in American Judaism had gained enough strength, especially in the Midwest, to justify the calling of a rabbinical conference to meet the new challenge posed by a forthright attack on Reform principles delivered, soon after his arrival in the United States, by Alexander Kohut. Kohut, an able and scholarly rabbi, had shown some inclination to moderate Reform in Europe, but his first series of sermons in New York City demonstrated clearly an intention to present a more traditional position.[29] Another relatively recent arrival from Germany, Kaufmann Kohler, replied to Kohut in his sermons and also took the lead in issuing a call to "all such American rabbis as advocate reform and progress and are in favor of *united action* in all matters pertaining to the welfare of American Judaism."[30] Kohler, a distinguished critical scholar of the Bible, had been one of the first Jews to accept the radical Graf-Wellhausen theory of the composite character of the biblical text. He was associated with the more extreme "Eastern" wing of American Reform Judaism. Although he consulted Wise and other more temperate advocates of Reform, the fact that the call was issued over his name made clear to all that any statement that emerged from the conference would take the "hard" line of Rabbi David Einhorn, Kohler's father-in-law.

Fifteen rabbis were present when the conference was called to order on 16 November 1885, at Pittsburgh. Others arrived later in the three-day session. Messages of regret were received from eighteen additional rabbis of Reform congregations. After the opening formalities were completed, Kohler read a carefully prepared paper that set the tone and task of the entire meeting. He spoke of the diversity of Reform motivations, opinions, and practices.

Looking at the various standpoints of progressive Jews individually or as represented in congregations, people only see that we have broken away from the old land-marks, but they fail to discover a common platform. . . . To many, Reform appeared the name for deserting the old camp and standard, while others beheld in it only anarchy and arbitrariness. Indeed, most of our so-called enlightened Jews welcomed the watchword of Reform as long as it meant emancipation from the old yoke of Law, but when it demanded positive work, the up-building of the new in place of the torn-down structure, they exhibited laxity and indifference. . . . It is high time to rally our forces, to *consolidate*, to build.[31]

As a foundation on which to build, Kohler presented a structure of ten propositions. With some changes in wording, Kohler's planks were hammered into the platform adopted by the Pittsburgh Rabbinical Conference. It is interesting to note that, although the Pittsburgh Platform was never formally adopted by any lay or rabbinical organization except the ad hoc group in attendance at the 1885 meeting, it became and remained for fifty years the quasi-official position of the Reform movement in American Judaism.[32]

The platform was ecumenical in character, asserting the sanctity of other religions and the dedicated sincerity of their adherents and welcoming interfaith cooperation with Christianity and Islam. At the same time, Judaism was recognized as *primus inter pares* by virtue of its presenting "the highest conception of the God-idea as taught in our holy Scriptures and developed and spiritualized by the Jewish teachers in accordance with the moral and philosophical progress of their respective ages." In common with a good deal of the rhetoric of Protestant Christianity in the late nineteenth century, the platform emphasized the social obligation of religion; it added that this obligation was traditional in Judaism, "in full accordance with the spirit of Mosaic legislation." The question of revelation was avoided; the word itself was never used in the document, and when its inclusion was proposed in discussion of the text, its use was rejected because of the ambiguities in interpreting it. The continuing value of the Bible was ascribed to its usefulness as "the most potent instrument of religious and moral instruction," and the description of the Bible as "the record of the consecration of the Jewish people to its mission as priest of the One God" supported the notion of Judaism as an ever-changing religion, "a progressive religion, ever striving to be in accord with the postulates of reason" (the last phrase coming straight from Immanuel Kant).

The position of the Pittsburgh Platform on the more theoretical issues was carried over with consistency into its statements on the more practical matters that lie at the core of the religious concerns of the average person. Of the three large questions that Kant had declared to be fundamental, "What can I believe?" is the question of an intellectual elite. "What must I do?" and "What may I hope?" are the concerns of the majority. Traditional Judaism, with its 365 negative commandments (What must I *not* do?) and 248 positive commandments, its ritual laws, its ceremonial laws, and its moral laws, provides a very full answer to Kant's second question. The Reform platform suggested a less taxing answer: only the moral laws of the Bible were to be regarded as absolutely binding. Of the other parts of the Mosaic legislation, the ritual and ceremonial laws, the statement urged that Reform Jews accept "only such ceremonies as elevate and sanctify our lives, but reject all such as are not adapted to the views and habits of modern civilization." Explicitly designated for rejection were the dietary laws and the regulations dealing with priestly purity and dress.

With regard to the third question, "What may I hope?" the rabbis in Pittsburgh assembled retained the doctrine of the immortality of the soul and rejected the beliefs in bodily resurrection and in punishments in the life after death. They transformed the particularistic and, indeed, nationalistic doctrine of a personal Messiah, who would be sent by God to lead the people of Israel back in triumph to a restored Davidic monarchy in the Holy Land, into the universalistic hope of a messianic age which would see "the establishment of the Kingdom of truth, justice and peace among all men." This transformation was accompanied by a rejection of the idea of Jewish nationhood, as nationhood had been understood in Western Europe and America since the eighteenth century. Thus the Pittsburgh Platform defined the Jews as "a religious community," and Judaism, by implication, as a religion among other religions. As Mordecai M. Kaplan has pointed out, this stand, like that of "the so-called Sanhedrin summoned by Napoleon in 1805 . . . virtually destroyed the image of the Jew by declaring religion to be the only bond of Jewish unity."[33] A more sympathetic account would say that these rabbis sought to strengthen the appeal of Judaism to modern man by reducing its ethnic stress and increasing its religious relevance.

The Great Migration

In the 1850s and the 1860s, some of the more extreme rabbinical leaders of the Reform group were arriving in the United States to join with moderate reformers Isaac M. Wise and Max Lilienthal in laying the foundations of a national movement. Bernard Felsenthal, David Einhorn, and Samuel Adler immigrated during the 1850s. Samuel Hirsch joined them immediately after the Civil War. During the same period, the traditionalist camp was strengthened, too, by the arrival in America of several German-trained rabbis, among whom Henry Hochheimer, Marcus Jastrow, and Benjamin Szold were outstanding. These three leaders, however, all held to the most liberal wing of traditionalism; Hochheimer might even be regarded as radical. The position they espoused was that of the "Positive-Historical" school of Zechariah Frankel, as taught at the rabbinical seminary in Breslau; in the United States this version of traditional Judaism has come to be called the Historical School and is claimed as the direct ancestor of the American-Jewish Conservative movement. In many ways, the rabbis of the Historical School were as open to modifications of Jewish practice as were the more moderate Reform rabbis. The stricter traditionalists, those inaccurately called Orthodox, were largely spearheaded by such unordained "ministers" as Isaac Leeser and Samuel Isaacs.

In the 1870s and 1880s, however, the resurgence of persecutions and pogroms, first in Rumania and then in Russia, led to vast Jewish emigration from those countries, many of the emigrants ending in the United States. So enormous were the number of these "huddled masses yearning to be free" that, in some years between 1881 and 1914, Jewish immigrants to the United States exceeded in number the total Jewish population of the country at the time of the Civil War. This massive immigration was the force that halted the trend to Reform leadership and offset the growing dominance of Reform Judaism on the American scene. For the new arrivals brought with them a type of Jewish piety that previous Jewish settlers in the United States had never known, not even in their Western European homelands before emigration. In Western Europe, by the eighteenth century, the Jews had already begun to be emancipated and, in part, assimilated to the surrounding culture.

The emancipation of the Jews of Eastern Europe had barely begun in the latter part of the nineteenth century. The Jews of that part of the world, to a very large extent, still lived out their lives in isolated enclaves, having minimal contact with non-Jews, though there was considerable secularization in urban areas.[34]

The newcomers brought with them their own communal traditions, still vigorous in Eastern Europe, though the Jewish community in Western Europe was of little consequence after the era of the French Revolution. They brought their own semisacred language, Yiddish, just as their German predecessors had insisted as long as they could on preserving the German language, and before that the original Sephardic settlers had tried to hold on to fragments of Spanish. There was, however, a vital difference between the linguistic conservatism of the earlier groups and that of the Eastern European Jews. For the new arrivals, Yiddish was not merely an ancestral tradition to be preserved out of reverence and in order to retain a tenuous connection to the lands of origin. It was, rather, a touchstone of Jewishness. As such, it served as a temporary barrier to the dangers of Americanization. The use of Yiddish in daily communication, the publication of newspapers and magazines in Yiddish, the development of a Yiddish theater, the carrying on of instruction in the religious schools and preaching in the synagogues in Yiddish—all of these contributed to insulating this group of immigrants from the currents of American life for a longer period than had been true of any previous group of Jewish migrants to the United States. It is only fair to add that, after the initial period in which Yiddish interposed between the immigrants and the American scene, it became a potent force for Americanization; but this development is tied to the history of the Jewish labor movement in the United States and to the emergence of naturalized East European Jews as a political force. Even today it is an advantage for a political candidate in some districts to be able to deliver campaign speeches in Yiddish. The transition is well illustrated by J. D. Eisenstein's note, in 1900, that "upwards of 20,000 Russian Jews massed together on the occasion of the last presidential election to read the bulletins displayed in *Yiddish* on a screen in their own Newspaper Row" on New York City's East Side.[35]

There had been a small earlier immigration from Eastern Europe. The first congregation following the Russian *minhag,* the Beth Hamidrash Hagadol, was established in New York City in 1852 by eleven Jews from Russia and one from Germany. Soon, several other Jews of non-Russian origin joined the group, presumably because they were unhappy with the more or less modified services in the synagogues to which they were affiliated. Abraham Joseph Ash, who served this group as minister, was probably an ordained rabbi, as were many of the Jews of Eastern Europe. It is interesting to note that two-thirds of the down payment, when this Russian-Jewish congregation bought a building for conversion into a synagogue, was donated by members of Shearith Israel, the Sephardic synagogue. Rabbi Ash, apparently, was not particularly pleased with his professional role; about 1860 he became a partner in a firm manufacturing hoop skirts, made a small fortune, and left his rabbinical office. When he lost his money, he returned to his congregational work. In 1876 he tried again, in the wine business; in 1879, this venture proving unsuccessful, he once more became rabbi of the same congregation, holding the position until his death in 1887. The willingness of the members and officers of the synagogue to rehire Rabbi Ash, despite his obvious preference for business and his constantly recurring quarrels within the group, is clear testimony to the shortage of rabbis of adequately traditional training and practice.[36] By way of contrast, it should also be noted that by 1900, less than fifty years later, there were nearly 300 Eastern European congregations in New York City alone.

When the massive migration of the period 1880–1914 took place, there was some increase in the number of Orthodox rabbis available for the vastly increased number of congregations, but scarcely any improvement in their quality. In part this may be attributable, as Charles S. Liebman has suggested, to the immigrants' being already more secularized than earlier studies had recognized. "Those who emigrated first can be expected to have been the least traditional, whose piety was at most what Leo Baeck called *Milieu-Frömmigkeit.*"[37] Rabbinical authorities in Eastern Europe did their best to discourage migration to the United States. One of the distinguished rabbis of Europe, at a public meeting of the Union of Orthodox Jewish Congregations, referred to the

United States as "this *trefa* [ritually impure] land." Rabbi Israel
Meir Hacohen (known as the *Hafetz Hayyim* [Seeker for Eternal
Life], from the title of his widely circulated book) urged potential
emigrants to remain in Eastern Europe in order not to endanger
their Judaism. Liebman notes as additional evidence for the
something-less-than-orthodox "orthodoxy" of the earliest Eastern
European immigrants that the "new immigrants conspicuously
neglected Jewish education" and the obligation to provide for ritual
baths (*mikvaot*). The evidence adduced in more recent studies
certainly suggests that the earlier accounts of the extreme religiosity
of the immigrants of the 1880–1914 wave were sentimentally
exaggerated.

Nevertheless, it is impossible completely to exonerate the majority of the religious functionaries who emigrated to the United States
with—or soon after—their flocks. They were, indeed, "improper
men," as they were called in 1887.[38] Rabbis, cantors, teachers,
ritual slaughterers, performers of ritual circumcision, many of
them with minimal qualifications and dubious credentials, flocked
to the new American centers of Jewish population. In the absence
of adequate supervision, they offered their services to the Jewish
public on a "free enterprise" basis, thus effectively defrauding
the poor immigrants both spiritually and financially. Not until
after 1900 was this situation even partially corrected; and only
after 1920 is it possible to speak of a properly controlled and
supervised functioning of orthodox Jewish institutions in the
United States.

If religious piety was thus in short supply among the earliest
arrivals from Eastern European Jewish communities, there was
certainly an ethnic "piety" that replaced it and served as its
quasi-religious surrogate. Jews in general were considered to be
superior people, an attitude transferred directly from the justified
sense of superiority felt by Eastern European Jews to the brutalized
peasantry of Russia and Poland. Russian Jews considered themselves
superior to Polish Jews, and, of course, Polish Jews reversed the
order. Within these broad groups, moreover, those who came
from each small community in Poland, or in Russia, thought
they were "better" Jews than those who came from the other small
communities. This is understandable; each small group felt lost in

the vastness of the new experience of America and defensively fell back upon its own local traditions, both to find an antidote of rootedness for the anomie of the immigrant and to boost self-respect by supplying it with an object of scorn.[39]

The huge number of small Orthodox congregations that grew in the first years of Eastern European Jewish immigration was unnecessary from the point of view of religion. The confusion and babble of tongues arose out of a cultural and social need, and took a religious form only because Judaism had traditionally been central in Jewish life. As a result, accidental and inessential cultural factors, such as modes of dress, styles of beard, or dialectal varieties of Yiddish, were retained with passionate attachment, while traditionally religious factors, like Jewish education, were permitted to decay. The orthodoxy of the immigrants was, as Moshe Davis has acutely noted, a "transplantation of culture." "If energies were squandered and hopes dashed in the effort to implant Orthodox belief and practice in America, it was due in additional measure to the stubborn refusal of Orthodoxy to reckon with the facts of American life and thought in the twentieth century—the very life indeed of their children born and raised in the new world. Orthodox parents still liked to pretend that the East European pattern of culture could be native to America, too."[40] Thus, even among those who were sincere and devoted in their religion, Orthodox Judaism in the later nineteenth and early twentieth century was more a cultural phenomenon than a religious movement.

In spite of themselves, the early East European immigrants made an important contribution to Judaism in the United States by introducing into American Jewish life a new sense of the relation between tradition and innovation. The Reform Jews, at this time, leaned toward innovation and sharply limited their practice to what they regarded as authentic and essential in the tradition. They were wholeheartedly involved in demonstrating the relevance of revitalized Judaism to life in the American world. The older group of traditionalists were far more sympathetic to the retention and preservation of Western European patterns of religious practice. Although they were aware of the need for adaptation and innovation to American ways and to the modern world, they demanded that any innovation of substance be justified and sanctioned in terms of the ancient tradition in the form in which they knew it. In effect, this meant that no significant change could be made. The immigrants of the period after the Civil War presented a third alternative, a strong inclination toward a literalist acceptance of traditional Eastern European patterns of Jewish living and, for many years at least, a reluctance to admit any innovation at all. Politically, the United States served them as a land of refuge from oppression. Economically, the United States offered a wide variety of opportunities for rising out of poverty. Religiously, however, America was a double exile: not only the traditional *Galuth* (exile) from the land of Israel, but also *Galuth* from the Eastern European substitute homeland, which they felt to be the only place in the world outside of Israel where a true Jewish life could be lived.

Isaac Leeser, for whom the struggle to achieve unity of Jewish life in America was a dominant passion, became convinced in his later years that there were two groups in American Jewry and that their reconciliation was most unlikely. In 1864, he wrote: "Much as all sincere Israelites must regret the possibility of separation, there can be no question that the evils of a declared severance will be far less than the fatal mingling of all sorts of ideas, in which the strict observance of our doctrines and laws is regarded as something useless in this age of vaunted enlightenment, in which everything is sacrificed to outward appearance, and reality is looked upon as far less valuable than a deceptive outside."[41] To those who followed Leeser in the dream of a unified Judaism in the United States, the picture must have seemed even less promising. For by 1900 it had become clear that the "severance" had to be threefold. There could be no common cause between Western European traditionalism and Eastern European orthodoxy.

3

Twentieth-
Century
Alternatives

The Protestantization of American Judaism

Except for a brief flurry of refugee immigration in the 1930s and '40s, the major elements of American Jewry had arrived in the New World before 1914. The story of Judaism in America since the beginning of World War I may be described as an account of the alternative modes of religious faith and practice that have developed within the enlarged Jewish population as it struggled to be both Jewish and American. The process of adaptation had begun for earlier arrivals at the moment of their landing in the United States; those of the Great Migration were destined to repeat, in terms of their own backgrounds, the experiences of their predecessors. The United States, too, had changed, so that what the Jews had been adapting to was not a static environment but a dynamic social order. Thus the needed accommodation can be fully described only in terms of the confluence and diffluence of two traditions, neither of which has a definitive creed.

Among all the alternative patterns of Judaism there is none that shows a total unwillingness to make adjustments. There are, however, degrees of readiness to make more or less reluctant concessions to the conditions of Jewish life in the United States. The ultimate norm of Judaism is not a creed, although there have been many Jewish creedal formulations; it is, rather, a mode of controlled change. Robert Lyon, editor of *The Asmonean,* suggested one side of this when he wrote of Judaism, "Although its principles are immutable, its customs are not." The difficulty that

Lyon did not face is that where there is no universally accepted creed and no central authority, there can be no final determination of what are "principles" and what are "customs." Dr. Kaufmann Kohler was on sound historical ground when he declared that "the Jewish religion has never been static, fixed for all time by an ecclesiastical authority, but has ever been and still is the result of a dynamic process of growth and development." Such a process, however, cannot be understood except in terms of a fixed point from which development is recorded and a regularly formulated law of change.[1]

In the demand for both a point of departure and a hermeneutic method there is a basis for differentiating the alternatives within twentieth-century American Judaism. A great many inconsistencies emerge in any such examination of the varieties, but this is inevitable. As Gotthard Deutsch of the Hebrew Union College once noted, "Inconsistency is the result of the unavoidable conflict between tradition and the requirements of the age."[2] The fixed point in Judaism, the point of departure, is not so much a set of principles, or creed, as a tradition. The method of change is designed to facilitate adjustment to the requirements of the age, taking that term to mean not only "the time" but also "the place." For the "requirements of the age" differ from country to country within the same time span, and from time to time within the same country. The laws of the Torah cannot be enforced with uncompromising rigor.[3]

Thus no single "American" version of Judaism has emerged. There have been many attempts to introduce some form of centralized control as a prelude to the development of a specifically American constellation of Jewish customs, ceremonies, and obligations. Even when these efforts were led by men of the highest caliber they have failed, because there were enough differences of custom as a result of immigration patterns and enough advocates of diversity to frustrate those who sought religious uniformity. This is not to deny that the Jews of the United States have acted, on occasions, in virtual unity. Unity and uniformity are by no means the same. Moreover, the occasional unity has come at times when there was a threat to Judaism, to the Jews, or, more recently, to the State of Israel. It has been a "foul weather" unity; when the sun comes out, each group again goes its own way.

As a result of the multiplicity of both backgrounds and visions, there are many religious options available to the Jew in the United States today. It is not merely that there are three major organized movements within twentieth-century American Judaism. None of these movements has been successful, even within its own affiliates, in fixing a uniform pattern. The three large "denominational" organizations are federations only; their powers are merely advisory, and their advice is not always accepted by their constituent synagogues. In addition, other smaller groups continue to exist independently, outside of the three large bodies. Individual synagogues, because they depend for their existence only on the good will and generosity of their members, are able to stand aloof and follow their own ways or, when they have been part of the larger whole, may secede from the corporate body in the aftermath of some disagreement of principle or policy. Judaism in the United States has been almost completely "protestantized."

Traditionalists All, Innovators All

Reform, Orthodox, Conservative, however much they may disagree, all agree in granting some force to Jewish tradition, and all agree in recognizing the need for change and adaptation. All are traditionalists, all are innovators, because the tradition itself allows for innovation. Nearly sixty years ago, Gotthard Deutsch summarized the American Jewish denominational scene in words that apply today, with some slight modifications:

The orthodox of modern type while adhering to the traditional principle in religious observances, as far as the ritual and the dietary law demanded, has quietly abandoned the stand-point of his fathers who condemned secular education and social life of the modern type. He loves instrumental music, he even tolerates vocal music, he no longer believes in the necessity of keeping up the tradition which demanded that the Jew should be distinct from his neighbor in appearance. The conservative quietly permits the infringement of the most rigorous Sabbath and dietary laws. He will carry and open an umbrella on the Sabbath, which once was a mortal sin. He would eat the bread of non-Jews, drink their wine and their milk. The liberal, the so-called reformer, will insist on the retention of [some] Hebrew in the worship, he will not miss the scroll of the Law written on parchment, he will retain the ancient formula of marriage and the Kaddish [memorial prayer] for the dead. Even the most radical stops at the Jewish calendar and avails himself of the religious force which "the days of awe" carry with them.[4]

Within the last generation, a considerable immigration of Hasidic Jews into the United States has taken place. In many respects, these groups are the most traditional of all American Jews in their practices, and have yielded least to their environment. Yet an article in the *New York Times* (23 June 1974) reports a striking attempt on the part of one Hasidic sect to use modern techniques of transportation and communication to reinforce traditional Orthodox ways and to restore spiritual significance to actions that have come to be performed as mere rote.

As loudspeakers played joyous Hasidic tunes, the [rabbinical] students—who study at the seminaries of the Lubavitcher Movement in the Crown Heights section of Brooklyn—patiently explained the spiritual meaning of [certain] devout Orthodox practices. . . .

The synagogue on wheels attracted curious Jews—young and old—at such locations as Broadway and 51st Street, Columbus Circle, City Hall Plaza, Broadway and 72d Street.

"They are our tanks against assimilation," remarked Rabbi Yehuda Krinsky, a top administrative official of the Lubavitcher Movement. . . .

The cavalcade had been initiated by Rabbi Menachem M. Schneerson, spiritual leader of the worldwide body of Hasidic Jews.[5]

Surely this is an outstanding example of a readiness for innovation in even the most traditional. At the other end of the spectrum, there are now groups of "Humanistic Jews" who reject supernaturalist beliefs, referring to themselves as "ignostic" [*sic*], who compose their own rituals without depending on the traditional prayer book, but who retain the Holy Days and holidays of the Jewish year. At least this much of tradition is present in the most radical of innovators.

Thus far this account has stressed the similarities of the various alternatives in American Judaism, those elements by virtue of which each may be called "American" and "Jewish." The differences are far more obvious, and far more crucial. It would be pleasantly simple if we could see an evolutionary pattern in the history of the Judaisms of the United States—if we could say that where Reform Judaism was in the nineteenth century, Conservative Judaism stands in the twentieth century, and Orthodox Judaism will probably arrive some time in the twenty-first century. There are, it is true, certain matters for which an easy generalization of this sort would hold, but they are limited in scope and do not adequately justify any predictions.

For example, one phase of the Reform movement in nineteenth-century America was the effort to overcome nonattendance at Sabbath services. A number of different devices were tried; some of these have been continued, while others were quietly shelved. The service was shortened; most of the elaborate medieval religious poems (*piyyutim*) were eliminated; some of the prayers were reworded to avoid expressions of Jewish particularism that might have been considered unpleasant or even offensive by sensitive and enlightened people. The prayer book was translated, first into German and then into a rather Teutonic English. A German or, later, English sermon was made a central feature of the service. Attempts were made to stimulate more decorous behavior during the services in the synagogue. A few synagogues replaced the traditional Saturday service by a Sunday morning service, because Saturday was a working day while Sunday was not; other synagogues supplemented Saturday services by Sunday services. None of these devices proved particularly effective. Then Reform congregations introduced the "late" Friday evening service, which rapidly became the most widely attended of all save the services on the major Holy Days. The proper combination had been found: an after-dinner gathering held in a tasteful and well-appointed synagogue building, a sermon by a rabbi who spoke English as well as—occasionally even better than—the members of his congregation, some part of the prayers translated into English, a trained choir, an organ, and some congregational singing. In skillful hands the Friday evening service became an aesthetic whole. What matter now if Saturday morning attendance was small, a bane of synagogues in the United States since the eighteenth century? The synagogue was reaching its membership on Friday evening, and to reach the membership means to retain significance in the lives of the members.

At almost every step in this process, anguished howls came from Orthodox and Conservative spokesmen. The Reformers—whether Isaac M. Wise and his moderate Midwestern rabbinical colleagues, or David Einhorn and his more radical Eastern group—were declared to be destroying the heritage of the faith. Sometimes the criticism was presented in general terms and the specific application left up to the reader. Thus, in the 13 March 1857 issue of the *Jewish Messenger*, Samuel M. Isaacs' editorial avowed that "if our religion be anything, it is as unchangeable as its source is eternal." True, only God can "fathom the belief. . . . But society requires some standard by which to judge its members. Hence various regulations have been attached to Judaism, obedience to which has ever been considered a test of man's religious consistency." At other times, the criticism took the form of an ugly and distressing personal attack on one of the Reform leaders, like the 2 March 1860 editorial in the same paper. Einhorn had written an article for the New York *Herald* in which he had asserted that views on messianic doctrine expressed in a then-recent meeting of the Board of Delegates of American Israelites should not be considered as representing the opinions of all the Jews of America. Isaacs' *ad hominem* reply said, in part: "Though [Einhorn] lives in America, his heart is evidently still in his native land on the other side of the Atlantic. He has no allegiance for anything American. . . . Having no nationality as an American citizen, it is not surprising that he should have none as an Israelite, and that he cannot elevate himself to that point which confidently looks forward to the fulfillment of the promise of a temporal as well as a spiritual restoration at the coming of the Messiah."

Nevertheless, in spite of the avowed and explicit opposition found in the conservative organs of Jewish opinion, virtually every move that the Reformers successfully introduced was taken over by Conservative Judaism, and in some cases by congregations of a moderate Orthodox stripe. To this limited extent it may be said that the Reform movement served as a pacesetter for all the Judaisms of America. In other respects the initial impulse to

innovation has come from supposedly more traditional groups. It
was in the Conservative movement that a newer and more modern
individualistic view of women's role in religious life was signalized
by paralleling the traditional initiation ceremony for boys (*bar
mitzva*), with a completely novel and untraditional ceremony for
girls (*bas mitzva*). There is no group in Judaism that holds a
monopoly on innovation; there is no group that has exclusive
possession of the Jewish tradition.

Reform Judaism in the Twentieth Century

Indeed, Reform Judaism, which in the nineteenth century tended
to an iconoclastic emphasis on innovation and, in many ways, a
rejection of the tradition, has illustrated, in the twentieth century,
a tendency to return to a more balanced attitude. In part, this
return may be merely an example of the "failure of nerve" in
twentieth-century society; even so, it is an important indication of
the degree to which the Jews and their Judaisms are part of the
larger whole, subject to all the stresses of world civilization.[6] There
are also reasons internal to American Jewish life. Thus, in the
nineteenth century, the Reform movement was virtually limited to
Jews of a Central European, Germanic background. The twentieth
century marks the beginning of the entry into Reform synagogues
of the second generation of Jews of an Eastern European background. Many of the Reform rabbis of the later period were young
men whose parents had emigrated from Eastern Europe. These
younger rabbis and their Eastern European congregants introduced
a different type of Jewish piety, less rationally formulated, far more
emotional in its expression, than the more radically rational and
"enlightened" piety of the founding fathers of Reform.

Many of the experiments of nineteenth-century Reform quietly
disappeared. In all but a handful of Reform congregations, Sunday
morning services were discontinued. An increasing amount of
Hebrew was restored to the service. More emphasis was placed upon
the celebrative aspects of the national holidays. Zionist ideas slowly
began to seep into both rabbinic and lay circles. Matters of this sort
are revealingly discussed in Abraham J. Feldman's *The American
Reform Rabbi*. Rabbi Feldman's experience in the rabbinate

extended back nearly half a century at the time of this publication. Characteristically of the Reform rabbis of his generation, he was born in Kiev, in the Ukraine, and came to the United States in his early teens. Thus his early years had given him experience of Eastern European Jewish life while his later American experience was in the Reform movement. Replying to a questioner, Feldman says:

I have changed some of the music of the Holy Days. They used to have all kinds of operatic music, and I wanted some of the old, traditional chants reintroduced. There are still people in my congregation (there are not many of them left of that older generation) who accuse me of leading them "back to Orthodoxy." . . .

I reintroduced, for instance, the *Esrog* and the *Lulav*. I introduced the Purim-eve service and the reading of the Megillah [Book of Esther], and a number of other things of that kind. Bit by bit, not all at once, these things were introduced, including such ceremonies as *hadlokas ha'ner,* the candlelighting, the kiddush. As these were introduced, I think our public worship has been considerably enriched.[7]

The resources of the tradition spoken of in this passage are, perhaps, not the most important to the scholar. They are, however, of the sort that is significant to the worshiper.

There has also been a tendency among Reform congregations to increase the amount of attention paid to Hebrew studies in their congregational schools. This may be a reflection of the slight increase in the use of Hebrew in the Reform prayer book. Rather more it is a product of the search, especially in the post-Holocaust years, for modes of positive identification with Jewishness. The Hebrew Union College–Jewish Institute of Religion, the seminary and teacher-training institution of the Reform movement, maintains a branch in the State of Israel, thus assuring a modicum of fluency in modern Hebrew among the newer rabbis. These, in turn, show more enthusiasm for a return to Hebrew in the services and for improved and increased Hebrew training for the children of their members. The process is therefore self-reinforcing, although there is scarcely yet a flood of Hebrew knowledge.

In the seminary, too, there has been a renewed emphasis on the study of Jewish law (*halakha*). The 1885 Pittsburgh Platform granted grudging recognition to "the Mosaic legislation" as "a system of training the Jewish people for its mission during its national life in Palestine" but declared that "we accept as binding only its moral laws. . . ." Some parts of both "Mosaic and Rabbinical laws" were specifically abrogated; those that "regulate diet, priestly purity and dress" do not "impress the modern Jew. . . ; their observance in our day is apt rather to obstruct than to further modern spiritual elevation." Present-day Reform is scarcely likely to return to the observance of the laws of diet, priestly purity and dress, but the rabbinical leaders have come to a more positive appreciation of the notion of religious obligation implied by the notion of commandment (*mitzva*). Repeatedly, in the sessions of the Central Conference of American Rabbis (the Reform rabbinical association), the question of formulating a *halakha* for the Reform movement recurs in the papers and discussions.[8]

On the whole, it may be said that the course of the Reform movement in the twentieth century reveals discontinuities with its nineteenth-century history. Very few of the leaders of contemporary Reform Judaism would still argue for the view that the Jews are no more than a religious community. The ethnic factor that their predecessors tried to deny is certainly no longer totally disregarded. Indeed, the 1937 "Guiding Principles of Reform Judaism" reintroduces a faint note of ethnicity by its definition of Judaism as the "historical religious experience of the Jewish people." Much more is said in the "Guiding Principles" than in earlier statements about "faithful participation in the life of the Jewish community as it finds expression in home, synagogue, and school and in all other agencies that enrich Jewish life and promote its welfare."

By 1937, then, the rabbinical body in the American Reform movement had tipped. It was no longer dominated by a majority of rationalistically and intellectualistically focused leaders of German Jewish origin. The practice of appealing and aesthetic forms of worship ranked with "moral and spiritual demands" in the new formulation. "Judaism as a way of life requires, in addition to its moral and spiritual demands, the preservation of the Sabbath, festivals and Holy Days, the retention and development of such customs, symbols and ceremonies as possess inspirational value, the cultivation of distinctive forms of religious art and music, and the use of Hebrew, together with the vernacular, in our worship and instruction.''⁹ This program, tending to a greater concern for traditional customs and usages, has not been accepted by all the Reform congregations in the United States, but the attempt to put it into practice is widespread and has given a fresh tone to the worship services in many Reform synagogues.

Conservative Judaism: The Sanctification of Ethnicity

Spokesmen for organized Conservative Judaism repeatedly suggest that it is a development of the "positive-historical Judaism" of the German rabbinical scholar and leader, Zechariah Frankel (1801–75). Frankel was a proponent of moderate Reform and a contributor to the "scientific" study of Judaism (*Wissenschaft des Judenthums*). From the 1840s, in reaction against some of the extreme positions taken by the Reform rabbinical conferences of 1844, 1845, and 1846, Frankel bent his historical scholarship to the task of defining a centrist position that did not reject the tradition to the extent that the Reform movement did, and yet took account of advanced academic and scholarly findings in a way that the Orthodox party did not. In both the Orthodox and the Reform positions, he foresaw danger to the preservation of Judaism. In criticism of Orthodoxy he said, "We must understand that there is nothing but disaster in that kind of absence of motion and deed behind which one looks in vain for certainties." Of Reform he wrote, "We shall conceive it to be our task to avoid the kind of negative reform which leads to complete dissolution." He hoped "instead, to show how the teachings of Judaism itself contain the possibility of progress."¹⁰

There can be no question that Frankel's influence was an important force in the background of some of the early leaders of the American Conservative movement and especially notable in the work of Louis Ginzberg of the Jewish Theological Seminary. So, too, was the contribution of Solomon Schechter (1850–1915), who was brought to the United States in 1902, in the reorganization spearheaded by Cyrus Adler, to be president of the Jewish Theological Seminary. Schechter was born and had lived in Rumania, and he had a deep sensitivity to the Eastern European style of piety. He had studied, however, in Germany, and had received an enlight-

ened, modern type of education; he felt intensely the "desirability
of adopting in our studies all the methods which distinguish
modern research from the mere erudition of olden times."[11] As
"reader in rabbinics" at Cambridge University, he had contributed
significantly to modern Jewish scholarship; his selections for the
Seminary faculty were guided by an appreciation of the quality of
their scholarship.

Apart from his own scholarly and administrative skills, Schechter
made a vitally important contribution to the Conservative movement by his formulation of the doctrine of "catholic Israel" (*klal
yisrael*), a doctrine that is easily transformed into the dominance of
the laity and which, on the intellectual side, is closely similar to
Frankel's view that Judaism is the religious expression of the "total
popular will" of the Jewish people. Either position can be used to
justify the retention of a particular traditional practice without
making the claim of supernatural revelation for it, or for changing
the interpretation of a scriptural passage without explicitly rejecting
the claim of supernatural revelation. Schechter's expression of the
principle, in two discrete passages in his *Studies in Judaism,* is
pellucid:

The norm as well as the sanction of Judaism is the practice actually
in vogue. Its consecration is the consecration of general use, or, in
other words of Catholic Israel.[12]

The Torah is not in heaven. Its interpretation is left to the conscience of Catholic Israel.[13]

Judaism, in any place and time, is what the Jews of that place and
time practice as their religion; Torah does not determine who is a
Jew, but the Jews determine what Torah is and says.

A third important element in the background of Conservative
Judaism is, then, the Jewish people. Not the enlightened intellectuals of the stripe of Frankel, Ginzberg, and Schechter, for whom
the ideas of the eighteenth century were "God-given truths,"[14] but
the refugees from late nineteenth- and early twentieth-century
pogroms and discrimination based on newer unenlightened European theory of "blood and soil" racialist nationalism were to be the
ultimate definers of Conservative Judaism. They were not the ideal

"people" of Schechter's vision. As Jacob Neusner has pointed out, this is a major weakness in the older conception of Conservative Judaism. "[W]hether or not 'Catholic Israel' existed in Schechter's day, it certainly does not exist today. There is no consensus, no collective conscience, and hence no authority to be located within the 'Universal Synagogue.'"[15] To put this criticism in other language, Conservative Judaism lacks a definition because the lay people are insufficiently united, either in practice or in theory, to be definite. Neusner's plea is that the Conservative rabbis and lay leaders undertake the task of definition. It is doubtful, in the light of Marshall Sklare's observations, whether there is any greater consensus among the rabbis in the movement than among the laity.[16]

Neusner and those other rabbis in the Conservative movement who call for a clear-cut statement of principles are voices crying in a wilderness of ethnicity. Jewish peoplehood, not Judaism, is what the Conservative movement is all about. One of Sklare's lay informants, in answer to the question, "What do you mean when you say you are Conservative?" replied, "I've been brought up in a very religious home and . . . have grown away from many of the customs. But I still have a strong Jewish feeling." This is an unfortunately typical response. Conservative Judaism, for its membership, is a way of maintaining self-identification and a measure of regard for one's parents' wishes or respect for their memory. This is particularly true of Jews whose European roots lie in Eastern Europe. Much of the popular strength of the Conservative movement is in the "gilded ghettos" of the Jewish suburbs.

The emphasis on democratic control of the Conservative institutions, on the one hand, and what has been a very traditional pattern of study in the Jewish Theological Seminary, on the other, have led to a perennial tug-of-war between the lay organization (The United Synagogue of America, founded in 1913) and the rabbinical organization (The Rabbinical Assembly, founded in 1919). On the whole, the positions taken by the Rabbinical Assembly are quite traditional; those taken by the United Synagogue tend to be more tolerant of deviations from the traditional norm of Jewish law (*halakha*). When the rabbis are pushed to accept changes in *halakha*, they do so with great reluctance.

A noteworthy recent instance is the question of the presumptive widow (*agunah*), the fact of whose widowhood cannot be established by the evidence required by rabbinic law—a situation bound to occur in times of pogroms or in modern war. The Conservative rabbinate spent a great deal of time—longer than the Orthodox rabbis—in reaching an accommodation to modern needs on this issue. On the other hand, it should be noted that far less time was needed for the Law Committee of the Rabbinical Assembly to reach what Neusner called the "painful and difficult" decision to allow riding to the synagogue on the Sabbath, for unless this decision had been reached, attendance at Sabbath worship, especially in the suburbs, would have reached the vanishing point.

Thirty years ago, one of the great voices of the American rabbinate, the late Milton Steinberg, sharply chided his colleagues in the Conservative movement. In *A Partisan Guide to the Jewish Problem,* he declared that "the leaders and official agencies of Conservatism have failed to live up to their preachments. Affirming tradition and progress, they have in half a century failed to commend a single departure, no matter how slight, from old patterns. For all practical purposes they might as well have been Orthodox."[17] Steinberg's criticism has been somewhat blunted by the actions of the Conservative movement during the past three decades. It is still true, however, that innovation is less eagerly pursued than tradition by the leadership of Conservatism, though lip service is often paid to the notion of adaptation to modern needs.

Reconstructionism: The Radical Form of Conservatism

Within the institutional structure of the Conservative movement, a smaller movement began some fifty years ago, composed of those who took the imperative of change seriously. Called Reconstructionism by its founder, Mordecai M. Kaplan, it has built up its own institutions, including a seminary, but has also acted as a leaven within both Reform and Conservatism. Reconstructionist Judaism is thus significant in American Judaism far beyond the number of those who are affiliated with it.

Paradoxically, the most radical proposals of Kaplan and his

associates spring from their very conservatism. The tradition of Judaism, through most of its history, has been to deemphasize and minimize the necessity of agreement with statements of belief, and to stress instead conformity to group standards of practice, both moral and ceremonial. Reconstructionism is an attempt to restore this ancient balance deliberately and self-consciously. As far as the conditions of modern life permit, traditional practices are to be maintained in their traditional form; the interpretations, or "rationales," adduced to explain and justify traditional practices are to be reconstructed in the light of current conditions and the current state of knowledge.

So, for example, Reconstructionists celebrate the holiday of Passover with a festive service and meal, as other Jews do. Through the years, the Seder has been an occasion of family and community solidarity. The interpretation in the traditional narrative (*haggada*) has been tied to the scriptural story of the Exodus of the Children of Israel from Egypt. The Reconstructionist *haggada* associates the same joyous ceremonial festivity with more recent events in Jewish history by viewing the holocaust years of the Nazi drive for a "final solution" of the Jewish problem as equivalent to the enslavement of the Children of Israel in ancient Egypt, and the ultimate defeat of the Nazis and the establishment of the State of Israel as the modern analogue of the Exodus and the arrival in the Promised Land. Reconstructionists would claim for this interpretation a vividness and authenticity that lends force to the identification of the individual Jew with the Jewish people. Reconstructionist leaders might add that nothing in this interpretation violates or contradicts what we know on other than religious grounds to be historically accurate.

Needless to say, Reconstructionist Judaism does not find it possible to maintain all the traditional practices recorded in the Bible or the rabbinic writings. Kaplan himself insists that an "objective and adequate rationale for Judaism of our day . . . has to select from the Judaism of the past those beliefs and practices which, either in their original or in a reinterpreted form, are compatible with what we now recognize to be authentic."[18] Among the traditional beliefs that Kaplan does not accept "in their original" form are the belief in the literal inspiration of the

Scriptures and the belief in a *personal* God. For both of these
central affirmations of the tradition of Judaism he has presented a
reinterpretation. It is doubtful whether all other leaders and
followers of the Reconstructionist position are as explicit as Kaplan
in rejecting these beliefs in their traditional form.

Kaplan has insisted on the humanity of the Bible (i.e., the Old
Testament, or *Torah*), not its divinity. He calls it "an expression of
human nature at its best, the most articulate striving of man to
achieve his salvation or self-fulfillment, and an expression of his
most conscious recognition that only through righteousness can he
achieve it."[19] He has drawn from Matthew Arnold a description of
God as a power in the universe, other than ourselves, making for
the realization of human ideals. This nonhuman power Kaplan
does not consider nonnatural. By his use of the word "God" he
means a natural power, part of the natural order of the universe.

A firm emphasis on the centrality of the Jewish people to
Judaism is the point at which Reconstructionist thought is most
closely akin to the Conservative movement. The Jews constitute a
cultural unit, a "civilization," within which their religion is only
one facet. Judaism is "the folk-religion of the Jewish people."
Often Kaplan reserves the term "Judaism" for the total phenomenon of what he has called the "advancing civilization of the
Jewish people."[20] Reconstructionism is most clearly a post-Enlight-
enment form of Judaism in its rejection of the idea that the
religious element can be separated from the rest of Jewish life, and
that it is an individual matter. In line with the sociological views of
the French-Jewish master, Emile Durkheim, Reconstructionism
interprets the Jewish religion as the expression of the group-
consciousness of the Jewish people. As a consequence, the more
aspects of the cultural life of the Jews can be fostered, the more
their sense of solidarity and their group-consciousness can be
stimulated, and the stronger their religious life will become. This is
the rationale behind Kaplan's assertion that "the spiritual regeneration of the Jewish people demands that religion cease to be its sole
preoccupation."[21]

Vital religion cannot be detached from the cultural matrix to
whose ideals it gives expression. Vital Judaism requires a vital and
dynamic Jewish culture. Group life fosters the development of

creative individuality because there is an organic relation between the group as nourisher and the individual as nurtured. To maintain vitality in the life of the Jewish group, its expressions must be translated into language that conveys both intellectual and emotional meaning to the modern Jew. Discussing the older supernaturalistic concepts, Kaplan writes: "Jewish religion has always assumed that, for man to maintain his God-likeness, he has to be the product of a people which orders its life in accordance with the will of God, or God-given Torah. That was the kind of people ancient Israel aspired to become." To be meaningful to the Jew of today as such a formulation was to the Jew of long ago, Kaplan says, its central idea and thrust must be reformulated in modern terms: "Built into the Jewish consciousness is the striving to have the Jewish People foster a type of civilization that is calculated to render man fully and divinely human."[22]

Orthodoxy in America: The Resurgent Remnants

The older orthodoxy of the first immigrants and their early nineteenth-century successors had largely disappeared by the beginning of the twentieth century. Its earliest stratum had been assimilated into the dominant American Christian community by marriage or conversion.[23] The later, largely Western European, traditionalists were absorbed into the Conservative group. American Orthodox Judaism in the twentieth century can be taken to mean the descendants of the Eastern European immigrants of the years 1880–1914. There is a small population of Sephardic Jews, who retain a strongly traditional attitude, but this group has not yet had a significant impact on the American scene. Another group of more recent German-Jewish refugee immigrants includes representatives of recent German traditionalism. This small group retains its identity, fusing neither with older groups of German-American Jews nor with the Orthodox of Eastern European extraction.[24]

Charles S. Liebman, a sociologist who has made a special study of the Orthodox Jews of the United States, uses for statistical purposes a definition of "Orthodox Jews as all Jews who are affiliated with nominally Orthodox synagogues." For Liebman's purpose, such a definition is not only valid but almost unavoidable.

Liebman's essay investigates institutional aspects of Orthodoxy. "For the most part, it ignores the doctrines, faith, and practices of Orthodox Jews, and barely touches upon synagogue life, which is the most meaningful expression of American Orthodoxy."[25] While it is undoubtedly true that synagogue life is most meaningful to the individual participant, and therefore of great religious importance, what part of this life is ethnic and social, rather than religious in the strict sense, is impossible to discover. There is a type of American Jew, as Marshall Sklare has observed, who may be called "non-observant Orthodox." He maintains affiliation with an Orthodox synagogue because he prefers to follow traditional patterns "when occasionally joining in public worship." He does not, however, live by the code of Jewish practice (*halakha*) that defines true orthodoxy.[26] Liebman has an extended discussion of this group and of possible reasons for its existence and its size.[27] He adds a further category of the "residual Orthodox," constituted by "those remnants of the East European immigrants who remained nominally Orthodox more out of cultural and social inertia than out of religious choice."[28] If these types are subtracted from the number of Jews affiliated in "nominally Orthodox synagogues" we are left with a "Torah-true" remnant of less than 5 percent of the Jewish population of the United States.

Moreover we must point out that even this small part is not united, does not constitute a precisely definable unity. It is composed, rather, of a number of separate remnants, each of which is firm in its members' adherence to an interpretation or a school of *halakha*. This is especially true of the several groups of Hasidic Jews, who make up the most visible segment of Orthodox Judaism because of their retention of Eastern European habits of dress and personal manner. Rather than being a denomination, even in the loose sense that this term may be applied to the Conservative and Reform federations of independent synagogues, American Ortho-doxy is a congeries of fragmentary sectarian groups, each one of which is itself composed of independent synagogues. Liebman's discussion of the Monsey area in Rockland County, New York, about thirty-five miles from midtown New York City, gives some sense of what this sectarianism implies. The "roughly 850 regular adult male Sabbath-attending worshippers and their families," almost all of whom had moved to the area after 1956, by 1965 were supporting no fewer than nine Orthodox synagogues, a Hebrew-speaking elementary "day school," a Yiddish-speaking elementary "day school," a Hasidic "day school," two high schools for boys and one for girls, Hasidic higher schools, and a school for advanced talmudic study with "a national constituency." The only local facilities in which almost all Orthodox Jews of Monsey are involved are "a *hevra kaddisha* (burial society), the local *mikveh* [ritual bath], and the two local Sabbath-observing bakeries."[29]

During the same recent period in which the Orthodox community of Monsey has developed, a period of approximately twenty years, one part of the Orthodox spectrum has moved toward the institutional and ideological stance of a denomination. This group, largely of those sympathetic to the Modern Orthodoxy that has become the hallmark of Yeshiva University, has at the same time begun to produce a literature that is not concerned with halakhic problems as such, and that, therefore, reaches out to the educated general reader among the Jews. In this way Modern Orthodoxy has begun to fulfill its mission to the non-Orthodox Jews. In addition, the Lubavitcher Hasidim, as reported above, have begun to develop a missionary thrust.

These examples of turning away from the self-seclusion of sectarianism have shown results, at least for the moment. Especially but not entirely among the youth and young adults, American-born, American-educated, and infected by all the doubts and questionings of modern social, political, and economic life, a significant number have translated their need to find a basis for stability into a serious attempt to live as "Torah-true" Jews. In their hands, what seemed to be a moribund orthodoxy has begun to take on new life. Shortly after World War II, the *New York Times* carried a series of feature articles on the religious revival in the new suburbs. One of those interviewed was the person charged with responsibility for stimulating the construction of Orthodox synagogues in suburbia. When the reporter asked whether there was difficulty in persuading the Jews of the suburbs to finance such synagogue buildings, the official replied that there was little difficulty. He explained that, whereas in the built-up areas of the cities the synagogues were already standing, in the suburbs people

had to erect synagogues before they could stay away from them.
Today the influx of younger people has partially stemmed the tide
illustrated by this anecdote. Resurgent Orthodoxy has become one
of the live options in America.

Moralism in American Jewish Life

In outlining the four major alternatives in Jewish life in the United
States, we have not exhausted all American variations on the
theme of the balance of tradition and innovation. Jewish Human-
ism has been mentioned only in passing; Jewish Science, despite its
nearly half-century of independent existence, has not been mentioned at all; the several varieties of Black Judaism have not come
into the account. All of these, and perhaps many other fringe or
fragmentary movements, have been available to at least a few
American Jews as the way of satisfying their spiritual needs. There
is, indeed, far more that might be said of the twentieth-century
alternatives.

The terms "Orthodox," "Conservative," "Reconstructionist,"
and "Reform" are merely proper names, not evaluations. A proper
name has a meaning, but not everyone who bears that name has the
qualities implied in the meaning. These names are conventional
ways of indicating a position on an axis, of which one extreme is
total rejection of the tradition, and the other extreme, total refusal
of innovation. Neither extreme is viable. There are, however, good
traditions and poor traditions; to call oneself a traditionalist is to
beg the most important question, the question of the value of the
traditions one supports. There are wise innovations and foolish
innovations; to call oneself an innovator is to beg the most
important question, the question of the wisdom or folly of the
innovations one advocates.

Meticulous adherence to every detail of ritual and personal
practice may be an expression of profound piety and moral concern
and of a keen spiritual sense of the sanctity of every experience of
every day. It may equally well be the husk of religiosity that remains
when the kernel of spirituality has rotted. A complete disregard for
the entire apparatus of ceremonial and usage may be merely an easy
release from committed obligation, or it may be the expression of a

set of spiritual values far in advance of those of one's contemporaries.[30] The danger of pride is ever present in measuring orthodoxy, and the danger is even greater in a relatively creedless faith like Judaism. Where there is no creed, there is no final statement of what is orthodox. To measure the orthodoxy or heterodoxy of others by setting up one's own views as an eternal standard is pride. It is far better to recognize that Judaism is many roads, all of which combine elements from the body of traditions with novelties reflecting the need of a new age.

From this standpoint, it becomes clear that there is another major alternative open to Jews in contemporary America, that of remaining culturally and ethnically Jewish while holding aloof from most of the organized religious activities of their fellow Jews. For this tendency, present in American Christianity as well as in American Judaism, the term "moralism" may be used. A complete and thoroughgoing moralism would involve the attempt to live entirely without religious institutions (or some surrogates). Except for a few people and for a limited time this is impossible. In the more modest sense used here, moralism will mean either the assertion that the primary expression of spiritual energies is the living of a moral life, or the assertion that spiritual energies may best be expressed through agencies and institutions that are not generally considered to be religious. Historically, Judaism has always been close to moralism in that greater emphasis has been placed upon the moral law than upon the ceremonial law.

In the United States of America, where people of all faiths have tended toward moralistic interpretations of their own traditions, Jews have followed the pattern in their own variety of ways. In the absence of adequate statistical data, it is impossible to say precisely how many American Jews have availed themselves of the option of moralism. To judge by the complaints of synagogue officials, the "unsynagogued" constitute a substantial segment of the Jewish population. One cannot speak of this class as having left the Jewish community. They are still very much a part of American Jewry in their own minds. They regard themselves, and are regarded by their neighbors, not only as Jews but also as *good* Jews by virtue of the time and energy and concern that they devote to doing good. Some are leading figures in Jewish communal and charitable associations and are held in high esteem for their services in such moralistic causes.

There are, of course, many among the moralistic Jews whose beneficent activities are carried out and whose spiritual concerns are manifested through organizations devoted primarily to the needs and interests of their fellow Jews. In many other instances, however, the concern is far more universal; it may be a concern for the victims of natural disasters, like fire or flood, medical disasters, like respiratory disease or muscular dystrophy, or moral disasters, like the rights of appellants before the courts. Whatever the worthy cause to which an individual devotes himself, one becomes moralistic when his devotion to the cause replaces devotion to the institutions of religion, and specifically to the synagogue, at the center of his life. That this should occur is neither unusual nor surprising; that it should be so readily accepted as an appropriate way of expressing Jewish spirituality is remarkable.

Not all of the unsynagogued are exemplars of a moralistic Judaism; there must be many who are genuinely indifferent to their heritage in the Jewish tradition. Furthermore, many Jews of all denominational leanings who are ardent supporters of the synagogues are also deeply involved in good causes both within and without the Jewish group. The lines of division are not rigid. The point is that there are a number of American Jews who express their religious feelings and satisfy their spiritual needs exclusively through social welfare activities, ethical causes, cultural creativity and stimulation, and even political participation in matters of concern both to the Jewish community and to the society in general. In doing so, the moralistic unsynagogued Jews pose both a threat and a challenge to those who are affiliated with the synagogues.

In an age such as this, when the dominant motivations of life are secular and this-worldly, to express religious dedication through secular service may prove increasingly attractive to the maturing generation, with a consequent loss of membership, income, and prestige to the synagogues. The challenge posed by this threat is for the synagogues and their members to do as much for the service and welfare of society as the nonsynagogal organizations do. Certainly from the age of the eighth-century B.C.E. prophets of righteousness and perhaps even earlier, the theme of social justice has been a major element in the complex fabric of Judaism. For many people today, young and old, the preaching of social justice seems the only raison d'être of religious organizations, and the striving for social justice the only meaningful form of religiously motivated practice. It is very hard for the well-established institution, religious or not, to keep the vision of social justice always in the forefront of its concerns. Platitudes about social ethics are much easier to produce than the fervent zeal and self-sacrifice without which the best of intentions produce but minimal results. The moralistic unsynagogued challenge the synagogues and their members to live out in full their ethical pretensions. This is a challenge that is difficult to meet, yet in itself it is a challenge central to the Jewish tradition. It is the link to traditionalism of the moralistic Jews. In the hierarchy of traditional Jewish conceptions of philanthropy there is a level beyond that of charitable giving (*zedakah*); it is that of charitable living, "deeds of lovingkindness" (*gemiluth hasadim*). It is to achieve this level that Jewish moralism challenges the members of synagogues of all degrees of traditionalism. In maintaining this challenge, Jewish moralism presents itself, without denominational organization, as one of the many alternative ways of preserving the living faith of Judaism in contemporary America.

4   *Zionism as a Religious Expression*

The Prehistory of Zionism in America

The course of Jewish spiritual life in the United States of America must be regarded as the product of two sets of forces interacting with each other. One set includes the complex of traditions that the Jewish migrant brought with him to his new home. The other comprises the conditions in the American cultural environment to which the immigrant has been forced to conform by his immigrant status or led to adjust by his own desire. Sometimes these two sets of forces have pulled in different directions, so that resolution of their conflicting demands has been difficult. At other times, in respect to certain issues, the two sets have been so closely linked that it is most difficult to judge which has been the more influential in setting the new direction of Jewish life. The emergence of Zionism as a form of religious expression among the Jews of the United States interestingly illustrates both of these patterns.

For many of the original Puritan settlers of New England, the notion of their own group as the new Israel was central. Their faith was strongly biblicist, and the frequent accusation of "Judaizing" brought against them probably means no more than that they placed great emphasis on the Old Testament history of the Israelites as the "type" of their own migration—their "exodus" from the "Egypt" of England to the "Promised Land," the "Zion," of the American continent. The imagery of "exodus," "travail in the wilderness," "promised land," and "Zion" served their need to identify themselves as the "chosen people." The Puritan sermons and religious tracts are replete with this biblical language, as is the traditional liturgy of the Jews. To the Puritans, needless to say, these terms were metaphorical; the geographic references of the Bible were used as images of their own spiritual situation. In this respect, the Jews were less clear; "promised land" to the Jews conveyed both spiritual home and explicit geographic location. Despite this difference, it is well to keep in mind the Puritan self-identification with the Israelites of the Exodus in attempting to understand the ambivalences of both Jewish and Christian attitudes toward Zionism.[1]

Proto-Zionist tendencies in the United States can be found in the early eighteen hundreds, with both Christian and Jewish writers referring to America as the land of refuge for the persecuted Jews of the world. In 1819, W. D. Robinson, a Christian, proposed the establishment of an agricultural settlement of Jews in the United States. Most remarkably for the time of Robinson's proposal, the very same era that bred the notorious American Society for Ameliorating the Condition of the Jews, Robinson's plan contains no hint of a missionary purpose. Indeed, Robinson seems to have been motivated simultaneously by a genuinely philanthropic intent and by a desire to speculate in western land.[2] After all, even better than merely to do good to one's fellow men is to enrich oneself by doing so.

At approximately the same time, a Jewish businessman, Samuel Myers of Richmond, Virginia (son of Moses Myers of Norfolk), conceived a similar plan. He communicated his plan in letters to a number of friends. Unfortunately, thus far no copy of his proposal has been found, but several of the replies he received have been preserved in the archives of the Myers family. From these, it is clear that Myers considered his scheme for a Jewish colony as a way of preserving the Jewish religion. At least one of his respondents, Joseph Marx of Richmond, held that Judaism could be preserved without the forming of a special Jewish colony. In addition, Marx argued, an exclusively Jewish settlement would reawaken anti-Semitic prejudices that might remain quiescent if the Jews were to be scattered widely among the general population.[3] Thus early, one of the controversies of later discussion was brought to the fore.

In both the Robinson and the Myers proposals, America was to be the "Zion" of Jewish settlement. The case is considerably more complicated in the series of plans and proposals put forward by the journalist, playwright, and politician, Mordecai Manuel Noah. In 1819, "Major" Noah proposed to the legislature of the State of New York that the state should sponsor a Jewish settlement on Grand Island, in the Niagara River opposite Buffalo. The legislature turned down Noah's suggestion. In 1820, undaunted, Noah wrote privately to John Quincy Adams, then secretary of state in the administration of President James Monroe, suggesting that Adams should send him abroad, ostensibly on some mission for the federal government but actually to recruit Jewish immigrants. At this time, Noah inclined to having the newcomers settle in a variety of places through the country rather than establishing a single Jewish colony.

Rejected again, Noah returned to his earlier plan for a "city of refuge" on Grand Island, but now he developed his ideas more fully. He decided that the city should be called "Ararat." He arrogated to himself the mouth-filling title of "Governor and Judge of Israel" and, in 1825, proclaimed to the Jews of the world "that an asylum is prepared and hereby offered to them" at Ararat. In this proclamation, for the first time in the documents, we learn that Noah intended Ararat merely as a way station on the road to the Holy Land, as a resting place "where our people may so familiarize themselves with the science of government and the lights of learning and civilization, as may qualify them for that great and final restoration to their ancient heritage, which the times so powerfully indicate." For Noah, then, there were two "Zions," the Zion of Ararat and the Zion of the land of Palestine. Neither of these Zions, however, was defined in terms of the classic and traditional messianic doctrine. With Noah, the religious view of the return as a supernatural restoration begins to shift to a secular view of the return as something carried out by human beings in their own behalf. Only in the latter view must the return be preceded by an interim process of learning how to run a government and how to live in the modern world.[4]

The further story of Noah's Ararat is an oft-told tale that need not be recapitulated here. More important for our purpose is to note that Isaac Leeser, minister of the oldest Philadelphia synagogue, Mikveh Israel, and later editor of *The Occident,* at this early period

(1831) still took the traditional religious view of a supernatural restoration and defined what he called Jewish "patriotism" as the continuing hope for miraculous return.⁵ Not until 1853 did Leeser endorse the idea of practical agricultural colonization. In one of two strong editorials in *The Occident,* after recalling to his readers the frequency with which he had brought appeals for the Jews of Palestine to their attention, Leeser wrote:

We need not be reminded that at present the hills are naked, stripped of the soil which once rendered them fertile. But we have read in a late publication, that they are limestone rock, and that it would not require overmuch labour, by breaking them up with spade and plough, to make them pay the husbandman's toil with plentiful crops of all kinds of farm produce. This is said to be the case even with the naked hills; but what shall we say of the fertile valleys, which now lie desolate, because there is no farming population to plant them? Other lands suffer because the population is too dense for their productiveness; but here is a spot situated in the centre of the courts of commerce, between the east and the west, weeping, so to say, because there are *too few* to satisfy its craving to nourish them. And who more than the Israelites have a claim on the soil of Palestine to obtain therein their support? Who, more than we, are better calcu-lated to draw the full benefit of Nature's bountiful gifts in our ancient patrimony? Many nations have borne sway over it; but it has not responded with its healthful products to their desire.⁶

A month later, Leeser carried on the same theme. He noted that many people had questioned why the Jews still clustered around the ancient shrines in the land where once they had been lords but now were little more than beggars. Where in the world, he asked, with the exception of America, Holland, Belgium and France, were the Jews better off?

Let us go where we will . . . the badge of political slavery and deg-radation is still ours. . . . Oh! what a freedom this is! What a state that is, to satisfy the longing of a Jewish patriot for happier days—for a time when the land of Israel is again to be ours, to be occupied by the sons of freedom and industry, sitting each under his own vine and under his own fig-tree, with none to

make him afraid! Whatever others may do, we do not blame
the oppressed, not even the free, in all lands, who look toward
their ancient home as the true country of Israel.[7]

The nations of Central and Eastern Europe were, to Leeser's mind,
the chief source of the colonists he envisioned in his dream of
freedom. He saw the Jews of America, as early as the 1850s, as a
source of financial support for the establishment of agricultural
colonies that would ultimately become self-supporting.

Two reasons may be offered for Leeser's shift from a purely
religious to a largely secular interpretation of the place of Palestine
in Jewish life. One is the reaction then taking place against the
small groups of perpetual pensioners living in the Holy Land;
messengers (*meshullachim*) traveled the world over, collecting
funds for the support of these poverty-ridden residents of Palestine.
As early as 1759, Moses Malki visited both New York and Newport,
and donations for Palestine relief were entrusted to him. He was
but the first of a long series of "messengers" to arrive in the New
World. There was some difference of opinion among the American
Jews about the desirability of this sort of contribution; while all
agreed that, for the maker of the contribution, it was a good deed
(*mitzva*), some felt that the effect of this form of charity on the
recipients was bad, for they were being encouraged to persevere in
their "indolence."

An extreme example of this attitude appeared in the *Jewish
Times* for 10 February 1871. "We have no doubt they are starving
[in Jerusalem], and the hungry is entitled by right of nature to
receive his bread from those who can give it. But have the majority
of these people any business to be there and starve? . . . Had they
employed the same amount of energy to reach a place where they
could find work and employment and a proper sphere for their
physical and mental energies, they would without a doubt, be
dispensers instead of receivers of alms." The virulence of this
statement is unusual; the sentiment is not. The Jewish population
of the United States was still struggling for its own security and
stability. An occasional contribution to help others make a start
toward self-sufficiency was not resented, but perpetual support for
those who made no effort on their own behalf was not to be

encouraged even on religious grounds: "As long as these pious fanatics are encouraged by other pious people, who merely lack the intensity of purpose and the courage to follow their example, they will continue to flock there. Starvation in their eyes is one of the steps to heaven. . . . That will not deter them as long as contributions pour in to alleviate their misery." Leeser, it would appear, was influenced by at least a mild variety of this impatience.

The second reason for Leeser's increased attention to colonization plans was that practical efforts were beginning to be made. Unlike the grandiose and possibly self-serving proposals of Mordecai Noah, several schemes that promised well were afoot in the 1850s. Leeser was aware, when he wrote the editorials quoted above, of the attempt sponsored by the "Agricultural Committee at Jaffa" to develop an agricultural settlement of Jews in Palestine. Indeed, the prospectus of this venture appears in the January 1854 issue of *The Occident*. It even named Leeser "chairman of the Central Committee in America" and authorized him to appoint local committees in every city in the United States where Jews live. Leeser was also aware of the plan of his fellow Philadelphian, Warder Cresson, to start an agricultural colony "near Jerusalem in the Valley of Rephaim."[8] Commenting on the prospectus, Leeser wrote that he could not decide whether to support the work of the "Agricultural Committee at Jaffa" or that of Warder Cresson, or both. He was certain, however, of the merit of the idea of founding such colonies in order to establish permanent stability and prosperity among the Jews in Palestine—"to restore . . . an honorable feeling of self-dependence and self-support, and . . . to do away with the necessity of constantly appealing for alms to feed starving thousands in our ancient patrimony."[9]

The story of Warder Cresson, whose projected colony Leeser considered supporting, is an interesting one. He was born in Philadelphia in 1798 and raised as a Friend, but became a religious seeker, passing through Shakerism, Mormonism, Millerite millenarianism, and Campbellite millennialism. In 1844 he went to Jerusalem, where he was to have served without salary as the American consul. Before he reached Palestine, however, his appointment was rescinded as a result of doubts cast upon his sanity by Samuel D. Ingham, a former Congressman and one-time

Secretary of the Treasury. "The consul has been laboring under an
aberration of mind for many years; his mania is of the religious
species."[10] In those days of slow communications, some months
passed before the rescinding of Cresson's consular appointment
caught up with him. While apparently serving as consul, Cresson
was visited by the British writer William Makepeace Thackeray,
who wrote of him, "His opinion is that the prophecies of the
Scripture are about to be accomplished; that the day of the return
of the Jews is at hand, and the glorification of the restored
Jerusalem."[11]

Thus it is clear that Cresson's volunteering to serve in Palestine
was tied in with his own millennialist reading of the Scriptures,
including the New Testament. By 1847 he was ready for conversion
to Judaism: "Upon the 28th day of March, 1848, I was circumcised,
entered the Holy Covenant, and became a Jew."[12] He decided to
remain in Jerusalem for the rest of his life, but first returned to
Philadelphia to settle his affairs there. In 1849, while he was in the
United States, his wife and son succeeded in having him declared
legally insane; on appeal, after a sensational trial, this verdict was
reversed.

Now Cresson (or Michael Boaz Israel, as he was renamed on his
conversion) decided that on his return to Palestine he would found
an agricultural colony outside of Jerusalem. This was the project to
which the sober and unimaginative Isaac Leeser gave serious
consideration. Abraham J. Karp wrote of this project: "Eight years
earlier Warder Cresson, religious enthusiast and U.S. consul, went
to Palestine to witness the ingathering of the Jews by divine means.
Now, in 1852, Michael Boaz Israel, devout and devoted Jew,
journeyed to the Holy Land to participate in the restoration and to
give of his ability and experience in planting on the land a 'hardy,
brave and independent population.' "[13] Karp interprets Cresson's
metamorphosis as one "from a curious observer to a philanthropic
Zionist" and finally to a settler on the land. This is a most generous
judgment. Considering the fact that only a few years later,
although Cresson remained within the Jewish fold, his religious
instability reasserted itself, a more balanced evaluation of his
unrealized plan for an agricultural colony might be that it was the
product of an interval of sanity in a life that had few such periods.

Zionism in America before Herzl

Early forms of Jewish nationalism were introduced into the United
States during the Great Migration of Jews from Eastern Europe.
Mass migration began in 1881; by 1882 there were already enough
Jews in America with previous association in the Hibbat Zion (Love
of Zion) movement in Russia to form an American organization of
Lovers of Zion (Hovevei Zion). The president was Aaron Simcha
Bernstein, editor of a Hebrew weekly newspaper, *Hatzofeh b'Eretz
ha-Chadasha.* Joseph I. Bluestone, later a student of medicine and
practicing physician, who continued his interest in Hebrew studies
and also served as editor of early Zionist publications, was the very
active vice-president of the American branch of Hibbat Zion.
Alexander Harkavy, who became an important contributor to both
Hebrew and Yiddish lexicography, was its secretary. Asher Ger-
mansky, a bookseller, was treasurer. Whatever fame these men were
destined to achieve, at this time they were young newcomers,
expressing through their activities in Hibbat Zion a sense of
continuity with their life before migration.[14]

The Hovevei Zion group established in New York City was more
successful than similar associations in other centers of Jewish
immigration. The natural audience for this group is reflected in its
leadership, all newly arrived immigrants from Eastern Europe. The
members of this potential public fell generally into two extreme
groups on the spectrum of Jewish religion. Either they were extreme
in their adherence to traditional beliefs and practices, belonging to
the most orthodox party among the Orthodox, or they were
completely secularized adherents of one or another form of social
radicalism. Each of these groups, out of its own deepest commitments, was utterly hostile to the Lovers of Zion. The Orthodox
rejected the program of Hovevei Zion because restoration, in their
theology, had to come about by divine intervention through the
agency of a supernaturally designated Messiah. The socialists
disliked the program because they had no patience with so
particularistic an objective as the regeneration of the Jews alone;
their goal was the redemption of all mankind. Between these
extremes, the mass of Jewish migrants were fully occupied with the
unremitting struggle to keep alive and had neither time nor energy
for larger concerns.[15]

About 1890, Dr. Bluestone, together with a number of associates (many of whose names are known, rather, by virtue of their children's later participation in Zionist work), formed a new organization, Shovai Zion (Returners to Zion). The members of this group aspired to purchase land in Palestine and to settle there. Their plans for settlement were never carried out, but the rabbis and journalists who were participants in the group kept the motif of agricultural resettlement of the Holy Land in the eyes and ears of the immigrant Jewish community. The Hovevei Zion, Shovai Zion, and other such groups, whatever their lack of immediate success, supplied a link between the prehistory of American Zionism and its later development.

The Impact of Herzlian Zionism

Soon after the publication of Theodor Herzl's *Der Judenstaat,* in 1896, American interest in the "new" Zionism began to grow, though very slowly. For years the Eastern European Jewish immigrants and their American-born children had supplied whatever "mass" interest there was in Zionism in the United States. The Jews of the earlier immigrant waves were, for the most part, indifferent or even hostile. Among the leaders, however, there were a few whose links were not to the Eastern European tradition out of which Hibbat Zion had emerged but to the Western Europeans with the same partially assimilated background as Herzl himself. Because Herzl had the attraction to appeal to Americanized Jews, such figures as Gustave Gottheil, rabbi of Temple Emanuel in New York City, and his son Richard J. H. Gottheil, professor of Semitic languages at Columbia University, were among the first American adherents of the new movement.

It was in Chicago, however, not in New York City, that the first *organized* Zionist society in the United States was formed: Chicago Zionist Organization No. 1. The group that met, late in 1896, at the call of the brothers Bernard and Harris Horwich, included "one lone member of the German-Jewish group," Rabbi Bernard Felsenthal. Despite the Gottheils, Felsenthal, and a few others, the Reform Jewish group as a whole was opposed on principle to Zionism.[16]

After the initial impetus supplied by reports of the first Zionist

Congress at Basel, the progress of Herzlian Zionism in all sections of the United States slowed down, although there was a steady, small increase in members of the new Zionist organization. Perhaps the most important step before World War I was the establishment in 1912 of Hadassah, the Women's Zionist Organization of America. Henrietta Szold, the daughter of Rabbi Benjamin Szold of Baltimore, was its creator; she was an imaginative, dynamic leader. Hadassah mobilized American Jewish womanpower behind the Zionist movement. Its corps of dedicated members worked not only in the community but also in their own homes to gain recruits to the cause. The vast energies that the culture of the age and the traditions of Judaism left so largely untapped were channeled by Hadassah into activism for Zion through the Zionist movement.

The Balfour Declaration of 1917 was an important crossroad for Zionist history in America. Until that declaration of the British government, the Zionist minority was on the defensive, forced constantly to justify its position and even to restate its raison d'être. After the enunciation of the declaration, although there was no immediate flood of American Jews into Zionist affiliation, the dynamics of the situation were altered. Now the neutralist or the anti-Zionist was the one who had to explain himself and justify his stand.

The Zionist idea, apart from its complicated relation to the traditional messianic hope of the Jewish people and Jewish religion, had always included two basic concepts—Homeland and Land of Refuge. These are of course complementary, not antithetical, concepts. From 1917 to the rise of Hitler, it seems fair to say that the value and stress placed on the idea of Homeland in the American Zionist movement outweighed that placed on the idea of Land of Refuge. For this reason a large number of American Jews who did not accept the notion of a Jewish nation (or even "nationality") could, in conscience, remain aloof from Zionism. Most communities of both the Orthodox and the Reform Jewish faith could, though for different reasons, remain religiously opposed to Zionism as a human effort to establish a national Jewish Homeland.

The rise of Hitler in Germany, the spread of Nazi racial doctrines outside the borders of the Third Reich, and the emergence—due in part to worldwide depression—of a virulent anti-Semitism led to a shift in American thinking about Zionism. The new emphasis on a Land of Refuge produced the greatest increase in Zionist affiliation in the history of American Jewry. In the classical institutional sense the wave of Zionist feeling and activity was not religious; indeed, it might well be called moralistic. The millions of European Jews were being subjected to policies of restriction, discrimination, and even extermination (the "final solution"). A whole nation was turning back the clock to a preemancipation outlook, and finding allies and support even in such bastions of modernity and of justice for the Jews as Great Britain and the United States itself. Something had to be done—in the first instance for the Jews of Europe, but who could say how soon the Jews of the United States might also be in need of a Land of Refuge? Zionism seemed to be the answer, at least for the immediate need. The moralistic zeal of the American Jew, whether Orthodox, Conservative, or Reform, or even unsynagogued, poured forth service and money in full measure for the relief of fellow Jews in Europe and for the building up of a Land of Refuge. Zionism became the true religion of the American Jew, and it was something of a revivalistic religion. Men and women who had for years scarcely considered themselves to be Jewish were converted overnight into passionate, active Jewish nationalists.[17]

Zionism as Spiritualized Ethnicity

With the sole exception, at least in recorded times, of the American Indian, every American is either himself an immigrant or the descendant of immigrants. For every American there are residual ties binding—and drawing—him to the land of his ancestors. The Irish-American, even after a century and more of life in America, still maintains ethnic solidarity with the "old sod." The Italian-American plays at *bocci* and dreams of the day when he will be able to visit the land of his forefathers. The Greek-American, the Chinese-American, the Polish-American, and all the other varieties of hyphenated American, including the Anglo-American, derive a sense of rootedness from continuing to use the language of their ancestral home, to eat the traditional foods, to celebrate their ethnic origins in all available ways—even, from time to time, to support revolutionary insurgency in the political life of the country from which their families migrated. This largely sentimental and easily caricatured ethnicity adds a valuable cultural diversity to life in America. More significantly, the ethnicity of hyphenated Americans provides all Americans with additional occasions for celebration, badly needed in an all too sober world.

Whatever else may be true of these ethnic groups, their festive occasions are not religious in quality. There are tensions between different ethnic groups within the Roman Catholic Church, but St. Patrick's Day and Columbus Day do not express these tensions. Jewish-Americans, however, inevitably spiritualize their ethnicity, for "Jew" does not uniquely designate a member of a people, as does "Bohemian," nor does it uniquely designate a member of a religious group, as does "Confucian." The Holy Days of Judaism and the secular holidays of the Jewish people merge into one another. A religious quality is associated with the newest of Jewish holidays, Israel Independence Day (Yom ha-atzmaüt), even as a national and ethnic motif is present in the holiest of Jewish Holy Days, the Day of Atonement (Yom kippur). The religious calendar of Judaism includes such national or ethnic holidays as Hanukkah and Purim, both of which enshrine themes not unlike that of Israel Independence Day, but from earlier times.

Of the alternative "denominations" in American Jewish life, the Conservative movement has had the least difficulty in adjusting to Zionism as a major theme in Judaism. From its earliest days as a distinguishable entity, the Conservative group has stressed the people of Israel (*am yisrael*) as the determining force in defining Jewish religion, rather than using an explicit definition of Judaism for defining a Jew. Early in the history of post-Herzlian Zionism there was some hesitation in the full acceptance of Zionism among the leaders of the Conservative group, because of the question whether Zionist affiliation implied dual allegiance, to both American and Jewish nationalism. Once it had been shown, partly by an emphasis on Zionism as cultural rather than political nationalism, that no dual allegiance should be felt, Conservative Judaism could accept Zionism as a central spiritual element in Jewish life.[18]

Orthodox Judaism had more difficulty in reaching an accom-

modation with secular Zionism. Although a small number of
traditionalist religious leaders in Eastern Europe had shown an early
readiness to accept the idea of human enterprise in the return to
Zion, the doctrine of a supernaturally commissioned Messiah was so
deeply entrenched in traditional Judaism that the vast majority of
leaders and many of the older followers were repelled by the notion
of a "political" return. Not that the traditionalists were averse to
resettlement. The ideal of returning to die and be buried in the holy
soil was, however, far more appealing than that of returning to active
agricultural work on the soil. A small fraction of the American
Orthodox community in the 1910s and 1920s formed the Mizrachi
organization; Mizrachi cooperated with the Zionist Organization
but retained its independence. Most of the Orthodox supported
the Agudat Israel movement in opposition to the striving for a
secular return. As among the Israelites of the Exodus, the division in
Orthodox ranks was largely repaired by the passage of a generation;
the maturing generation of the young overwhelmingly endorsed the
Mizrachi position, and the Agudah became a tiny group of older
people with virtually no support in the United States. In 1957,
Mizrachi and its fellow Orthodox Labor-Zionist movement, Hapoel
Hamizrachi, united in the Religious Zionists of America. Its
activities in Israel include support of the National Religious Party, in
the political field, and of a variety of philanthropic causes. On the
American front, the organization supports educational programs
and a number of publications in English, Hebrew, and Yiddish. Of
other Orthodox groups that support religious Zionism it is perhaps
most important to mention Young Israel, a movement that began in
1912 among a group of young people who retained their parents'
adherence to Orthodoxy but considered some of the Eastern
European customs inappropriate to an American setting. From the
beginning, Young Israel has been pro-Zionist, and its members
today are likely to be active in the Religious Zionists of America.

The course of Zionism in Reform Jewish circles was even more
complicated. From its nineteenth-century German beginnings,
Reform Judaism had followed the logic of early theories of Jewish
emancipation by a deliberate negation of Jewish nationhood. Jews
were to be Germans (or Frenchmen, or Americans) of the "Mosaic
persuasion." In the United States, the Pittsburgh Platform of 1885

explicitly set forth this renunciation: "We consider ourselves no longer a nation but a religious community, and therefore expect neither a return to Palestine, nor a sacrificial worship under the administration of the sons of Aaron, nor the restoration of any of the laws concerning the Jewish state." The *Hebrew Union College Journal* added its voice to the swelling chorus in 1896: "We have warmly, and earnestly enough, held that the Jews are not a nation. In accordance with this view, we have allowed the purely national holidays of Judaism to drop into the background and have expurgated the prayers for return to Jerusalem from the ritual of others." Oscar and Mary Handlin summarize the ongoing movement: "The Union of American Hebrew Congregations proclaimed, 'America is our Zion,' and the Central Conference of American Rabbis in 1896 and '97 and again in 1912 and '17 had specifically condemned the Zionist program."[19]

In spite of this explicit renunciation of the national aspirations of the Jewish people, and in spite of the overwhelming internal drive in the Reform group, during and after World War I, to "Americanize," a number of rabbis and well-established German-Jewish laymen entered with enthusiasm into the nascent Zionist movement. Even such a thoroughly secularized and assimilated Jew as Justice Louis Dembitz Brandeis was drawn into Zionist activity. Through the 1920s, almost every plenary meeting of the (Reform) Union of American Hebrew Congregations or of the (Reform) Central Conference of American Rabbis was marked by an effort to modify the anti-Zionist stand of the Reform movement. The efforts were unsuccessful, however, even though the personal views of rabbis and laity were increasingly pro-Zionist.

Not until the 1930s did the balance begin to tip. Where the themes of Homeland and national self-determination were unavailing, the themes of Land of Refuge for the oppressed and persecuted, and of ethnic solidarity, were effective. In the 1935 convention of the Central Conference of American Rabbis, the confrontation between the older and the younger points of view emerged clearly in the debate between Samuel Shulman and Abba Hillel Silver. The changed climate was manifest. Rabbi Shulman sought to salvage the remnants of what had earlier been a firm consensus of antinationalism; bringing his splendid resources of

knowledge and oratorical skill to bear, he pleaded, in effect, to retain
the link with the earlier Reform movement. Rabbi Silver, still a
relatively young man but already a leader in American Zionist circles,
rode the crest of a new wave; he spoke as one who knew that the
majority of his auditors supported him. Yet it was not until 1937 that
the Union of American Hebrew Congregations affirmed "the
obligation of all Jewry to aid [in building Palestine] as a Jewish
homeland by endeavoring to make it not only a haven or refuge for
the oppressed but also a center of Jewish culture and spiritual life."
In the same year, in the Columbus Declaration of Guiding Principles
of Reform Judaism, while reaffirming the characteristic position that
Judaism is a religious community, the Reform rabbis left the decision
on Zionism up to the individual congregation. Not until 1943 was
there an explicit acknowledgment of the compatibility of Zionism
and Reform Judaism.

American Zionism after Israel's Independence

From the mid-1930s to 1948, Zionism was the chief element in the
living faith of the vast majority of American Jews. For some, Zionism
was a cause embraced in addition to synagogue affiliation. Others
used their commitment to Zionism as a substitute for overtly
"religious" affiliation. During these years between the rise of Hitler
and the independence of the State of Israel, Zionism was not only a
vital and dynamic factor in American Jewish life; many considered
the establishment of a Jewish National Home and Refuge "the thing
that mattered most." In 1945, a poll by the Roper organization
showed that nearly 90 percent of all American Jews were supporters
of Jewish settlement in Palestine. Even most opponents of such a
settlement may be said to have raised their committed opposition,
on a principled basis, to the level of religious faith; certainly
anti-Zionism was the most vital factor in their spiritual life. On both
sides, the cause attracted intense devotion and depth of feeling.
Conservative Rabbi Israel Goldstein's ecstatic proclamation expressed the feelings of many American Jews: "Palestine is the
heart of Jewish hope and promise. Zionism is the spiritual dynamic
of the Jewish people. It helps to give spiritual content to Jewish life
everywhere. Zionism offers the guarantee that when democracy will

triumph in the world, Judaism will not melt away under the sun of freedom. It is the supreme expression of the mystic will to live which is the stubborn fact of Jewish history."[20]

This is the story, at least until *atzmaüt* (independence). So intense was the support of American Jews for the settlers that in 1948, when the partition plan for Palestine was a major issue in the international politics of the day, virtually the entire Jewish population of the United States became a monolithic pressure group in support of the Zionist objectives. The Synagogue Council of America, an organization that crossed every line of division in American Jewry, called for a day of prayer, 8 April 1948, "to give expression to the shocked conscience of America at the inexplicable action of our Administration in reversing its Palestine policy [by no longer supporting the partition plan, and] to demand the fulfillment of the plighted word of this country and of the nations of the world, and to pray for God's help."[21]

Though many American Jews have been leaders in the world Zionist movement, the relations between American Jewry, even its Zionist group, and world Zionism have not been free from tension, friction, and occasional hostility. A third protagonist, since 1948, has been the government of the State of Israel. Each of the three—the Israeli government and the American and international Zionist movements—is dedicated to the same end, but each plays a different part. The reasons for friction and resentment are inherent in the situation.

The American Jew, in general, no matter how passionately he may talk of Israel as Homeland (*eretz*), really considers the United States as *his* homeland. Israel is to be the homeland of Jews from other parts of the world. He feels "at home" in America, even though he knows that in the technical language of Jewish religion America is still a land of exile (*galut*). Indeed, one of the Israeli resentments is that, in the mass, American Jews have never thought of themselves as potential settlers in Israel. Israel is for Jews from lands of oppression. Israel is Land of Refuge. The free Jew of the United States supports the State of Israel with his devotion, his time, his labor, his money, and, all too often, his advice, but not with himself, save as an occasional visitor. There are, of course, individual exceptions, but the greater number of American Jews have no desire to be more than

tourists in Israel. There has been, however, an increase in the number
of American immigrants to Israel since the Six-Day War of 1967.
Sideline criticism and Monday morning quarterbacking have
naturally occurred. The American Jew, Zionist or not, who does not
have to live with the day-to-day political, social, economic, and
military problems of Israel, inevitably fails to understand the reasons
for some of the policies that are followed by the Israeli government.
The American cannot comprehend why the State of Israel accepts
compromises where he would stand firm, and is intransigent where
he would be willing to yield. He grows impatient; he is full of
suggestions of what he would do, in a situation about which he does
not have enough information to evaluate. Understandably officials
of the Israeli government, confronted with very delicate internal as
well as international situations, resent the attempt of the Americans
to intrude into policy decisions.[22]

A newer element in the total picture, the consequences of which
are not yet clear, is the development in the American "New Left" of
an intensely anti-Israel spirit. How far and for how long the
universalistic appeal of the leftist position will influence a large
number of Jewish young people cannot be foreseen. To the extent
that Israel is now, and will be for a long time, dependent upon the
financial support of the Jews of the United States, the defection of
the Jewish fragment of the New Left could become a very serious
matter within a few years. Marshall Sklare, whose observation of this
phenomenon of alienation is both keener and more dispassionate
than most, has commented that "in the extreme New Left version
of the Middle East conflict Israel is regarded as an imperialist nation
bent on subverting progressive Arab regimes. In a more mild
interpretation Israel is regarded as an ally and tool of American
imperialism. Consequently American Jews who support Israel are
guilty of supporting American foreign policy. Thus in contrast to the
old fear that Jews who support Israel would be regarded as disloyal to
America, Jews who support Israel are now being charged with loyalty
to America."[23]

In times of crisis, like the Six-Day War of 1967 or the Yom Kippur
War of 1973, the ambivalences in the relations of American Jews and
Israelis tend to be submerged. All differences of opinion and
reservations concerning policy are subordinated to a wartime

unification. When the crisis situation eases, the ultimate difference reemerges. For the Jews of America, the State of Israel is the current form of the religious dream of two millennia and more; for the Jews of Israel it is a secular state with all the economic, social, and political problems of a developing nation. Between 1933 and 1948 this basic antithesis could be overlooked; for shorter periods since 1948 it had to be disregarded. But the difference remains.

5 Individual and Community: Affiliation and Disaffiliation

Synagogue or Community?

In our times, when the question of affiliation is raised in a Jewish context, the information usually sought is what proportion of the Jewish population in any particular geographic area holds membership in the synagogues of that area. The urgency of keeping the synagogues going, paying the salaries of professional and nonprofessional employees, retiring the mortgage, and maintaining religious schools and other service functions of the synagogues is the constantly pressing, and often depressing concern of local communities and, at times, even of the larger community. Synagogue affiliation nowadays, and particularly in the United States, seems to most of us to be the natural—the necessary—interpretation of Jewish affiliation. Affiliation means synagogue membership and support. Nonaffiliation means failure to support a synagogue.

In the perspective of history, this focus on the synagogue is a relatively recent and perhaps unfortunate innovation. The basic unit of Jewish organization throughout most of Diaspora history was not the synagogue but the community. Jewish affiliation meant attachment to the community. The community, through its subordinate agencies, maintained all the service functions that were needed to keep its members going or, since cemeteries were included, to keep its late members gone. The establishment and staffing of synagogues was itself one of the service functions of the Jewish community. Not in absolute terms, but in a relative sense, the affiliation of the Jews to the Jewish community was a natural and organic coherence, whereas the attachment of Jews today to the synagogues is an artificial and mechanical adherence. The difference is in some ways comparable to the differing relations that a man has to his mother and to his wife respectively. Mother and son are tied together in an organic, coherent bond that even death does not dissolve, whereas a man and wife are joined together by a mechanical link, because a marriage is always terminable.

There is an interesting, if minor, point that should be recalled about the Jewish situation in the American colonial world, before the establishment of the United States of America. The very first formal association of the Jews of New Amsterdam was not to found a synagogue, but to create and administer a cemetery. It was a communal function rather than a synagogal function. There is no doubt, despite the absence of recorded evidence, that the Jews of New Amsterdam gathered earlier as a *minyan* for purposes of prayer, but that is not the same as a synagogue. When formal groupings of Jews began to be established in the British-American colonies, in Philadelphia, New York, Charleston, and Newport, they probably thought of themselves primarily as attempts to organize Jewish communities—that is, to span and regulate the total life of the Jews rather than to be specialized religious institutions—though their organizations, for various discoverable reasons, took the form of synagogues. At the very same time, however, that Jews in the various cities were founding these groups, they were also, unintentionally, setting in motion forces that pointed in a direction away from such overall Jewish community structure. In part, we can ascribe this to the opportunity that the Jews had, and were well aware that they had, in a new land, to be on a par with their fellow residents from the very beginning of settlement. A separatist attitude, such as would have been manifested by a reduplication of the European Jewish community on American soil, would have implied a desire for special status. So, for example, the Jews of New Amsterdam early struggled for the right to an equality of service with the whole colony, the right to share with their non-Jewish fellow residents the difficult, possibly dangerous chore of guard duty against hostile raids of Indians or, possibly, British troopers. The earlier military participation of the Sephardim in Spain might have prepared them, but the reason they fought for and won this right was not to gain any privilege but rather to avert any pattern of discrimination.

Again, Jews in the eighteenth century particularly, but also on into the nineteenth and twentieth centuries, have been very active in Freemasonry in America. The early activity of Jews in Freemasonry constitutes clear evidence of a determination to be socially unified with their non-Jewish fellows. It shows a desire not to develop as a separate, segregated Jewish social body. After 1843 it was possible for the same Jew to be a member of a Jewish fraternal order like B'nai B'rith and also to be a Mason. Masonic groups participated in such intra-Jewish occasions as the dedication of new synagogues and Jewish funerals.[1] The insistence on guard duty and the readiness to associate with non-Jews in groups like the Masons is evidence that from the very beginning of Jewish inclusion in the settlement of the American continent, the Jews were resolved to be fully part of a society that we would call "pluralistic." They, of course, did not know that word; it is a modern coinage.

The strength of the Jewish community in Europe had been that, except for the possibility of conversion to Christianity, an individual Jew had no alternative save to accept the rules and guidelines laid down by Jewish communal authority.[2] He was born into the orbit of the Jewish community; he was educated in it; he married in it; he raised his own children in it; he died in it; he was buried in it. From womb to tomb he was the creature of the community. If, in order to escape, he converted to Christianity, in many places in Europe he found himself a pariah, an outcast, at least socially. By his conversion he abandoned his relation to those who had previously been his fellows in the Jewish community, but because the Christian community never really trusted those whom they called New Christians, he was seldom able to enter into a mutually supportive relation with Christians. Moreover, until the period of the Enlightenment, European society had little place for the isolated individual, especially the isolated Jew. A rare intellectual type like Spinoza could manage, in great measure, to go it alone, although we must remember that even Spinoza had a society of correspondents, with whom he maintained communication through letters. The tragic life of Spinoza's near-contemporary, Uriel da Costa, shows plainly how unusual Spinoza's case was. Nonaffiliation was all but impossible, and consequently, of course, affiliation was unavoidable.

Individualism, in the form in which we know it, is a recent

phenomenon in social history. Born or adopted, as all of us have been, into an individualistic society, the notion of an individual who transcends the group, who has rights beyond his membership in a group, is so natural to us that we can scarcely conceive that in the Middle Ages there was no such thing as "the Individual." One's identification of himself to himself, as well as his identification by others, was expressed in terms of a complex of relationships. To some extent, in practice if not in theory, the same situation holds even now. We identify ourselves to others in a variety of ways that are institutional and organizational, not individual, but we ourselves lose sight of their corporate character. In the more impersonal settings of our daily life, we should find considerable difficulty in identifying ourselves to others without showing membership cards, licenses, privilege cards, credit cards, and Social Security numbers. Even today, then, corporate identification lies implicitly behind my identification of myself, although explicitly and consciously I think of myself as this particular person, this identity, this Individual.

For many reasons, the social pattern of corporate identification that had been the norm in Europe practically to the beginning of the nineteenth century did not become dominant in America, except with regard to one group, the Blacks. Identified in the past in the traditional European "status" way, Blacks now justifiably want to be identified as individuals, like the rest of us. Most religious groups in America from colonial times almost to the present day, have been organized not in the traditional way but on a voluntary basis. They have not made energetic attempts to restrict or monopolize the social life of their adherents. Since about the time of America's entry into the Second World War, any attempt on the part of religious groups to dominate the social life of their members has been breaking down. From this general statement we must exempt specifically communitarian groups, such as some eighteenth-century Baptist groups that settled in Pennsylvania or nineteenth-century groups like the Mormons who settled farther to the west. In large measure, however, the settlement of the United States was carried out not by groups but by strong individualists, or by family groups dominated by strong individualists.[3]

This sort of temper, rather than the rigidities, the fixed relationships, of the European social scene, was what the Jews encountered when they came to the United States in the early days. In addition, those Jews who braved the terrors of the sea voyage and the rough unknown of America were not the more timorous and less enterprising temperaments who sought the continued security of life in community, but precisely those whose own dispositions were suited to the rugged openness of American conditions.[4] It is no wonder, then, that the problem of the "unsynagogued" had already raised itself in the eighteenth century. The minutes of New York's oldest congregation, Shearith Israel, for the mid-eighteenth century, contain references to unsynagogued, unaffiliated Jews and report the efforts of the synagogue's officers and board to discover ways of bringing the unaffiliated back into the fold, out of concern both for the future of Judaism and for the support and maintenance of the synagogue.

Similar problems and personalities worked to prevent the emergence, on any more than a temporary basis, of an overarching community structure for American Jewish life, in spite of the best efforts of many Jewish leaders. It should be noted that in most of the colonies on the Eastern Seaboard the dominant religious groups were Protestant, and that most of these Protestant churches were organized by congregational units. As a result, the first laws respecting charters for religious organizations, from the New England states all the way south through Maryland, were phrased in such a way as to encourage the chartering of separate congregations rather than associations of congregations. When Roman Catholics began to appear in sufficient numbers in New York State, they had to have a special amendment put through the state legislature to enable them to organize in the way to which they were accustomed. Otherwise the Protestant congregational form of organization, with property control vested in lay representatives, would have been the only one that they could have legally used.

The Jews of that era were not numerous enough to press for a special amendment, even if a majority had wanted to do so. It must be remembered that we have been talking of colonial days or of the early national period of American history, when the entire number of Jews in the United States was extremely small and the annual increase by immigration scarcely noticeable. There are city blocks in New York City, Chicago, or Boston today where more Jews live than there were in all of America in 1790. Immigration did not increase substantially until after 1840, and then it came in two very unequal waves. The earlier and smaller wave of Jewish immigration from Western Europe, particularly Germany, began in the late 1830s and slowly gathered momentum, reaching its peak in 1848 and the years immediately following. It included a very few German Jews who had been involved in the revolutionary movements of the time and who, after the failures of 1848, decided that their best bet was to get out. After 1850, this stream of immigration began to subside and had died out almost completely at the time of the Civil War.

Then there was a much larger wave of Eastern European Jews, beginning in the 1870s with Rumanian immigration, and swelling in the 1880s with a mass movement out of Russia. This flood continued right up to 1914, when it was cut off by World War I. After the war, when immigration might otherwise have resumed, the Congress of the United States passed severely restrictive immigration laws which dammed the potential flood to a tiny trickle.

Both the German Jews and the East European Jews, unlike their predecessors, often arrived in the United States in community groups, or sent over a few men to prepare the way and then followed in larger numbers as soon as it was financially possible for them to do so. There were instances in which two-thirds to four-fifths of a small German Jewish community immigrated as a body. In addition to their group migration pattern, these later arrivals were far more accustomed to living within the confines of a Jewish community than the earlier immigrants had been. Fewer of them had the spirit of the independent pioneer.

Moreover, not long after the beginning of the larger, Eastern European wave, for the first time in American history a significantly anti-Semitic frame of mind began to manifest itself. Isolated cases of prejudice can be found earlier, but widespread anti-Semitism is not discoverable before about 1890, and this late nineteenth-century development occurred not only among non-Jews but also among the Jews who were already well established on the American scene. American anti-Semitism, though often associated with Populism, was not basically ideological. It was, rather, part of the visceral xenophobia that characterized American life in the late nineteenth century as a consequence of the increased proportion of "ethnics" in the population. Faced with the need to retain the cohesiveness of the Jewish group in spite of this antagonism, and with the increasing number of immigrant Jews arriving in groups from long established communities, American Jewry might have been expected to develop a more strongly communal pattern. Such a pattern did not emerge, however, because the central element in Jewish identification ceased to be membership in a Jewish community and became, instead, affiliation with a synagogue.[5]

The Jews who came to the United States after 1870 came from many different sections of the various countries of Eastern Europe. They brought with them traditions of Jewish practice that had very ancient sanctions. But these traditions had all been modified to a greater or lesser degree by the local European environment in which particular Jewish groups had lived. The semisacred language of Yiddish has become more sacred today than it was seventy or eighty years ago, because fewer people use it today, but even in those days it was already a semisacred language. However, it manifested dialectal differences from place to place, so that while a Yiddish-speaking Jew from Rumania and a Yiddish-speaking Jew from Lithuania could understand and presumably communicate with each other, by using different dialects of the same language they could recognize their "otherhood" as well as their brotherhood. A common language provides a basis for misunderstanding at least as often as a basis for understanding. Similarly, certain modes of dress that originally had no association whatsoever with the traditions of Judaism had developed a semisacred character and were used by some groups as touchstones of Jewishness.

In addition to such relatively external matters as dialect and customary dress, there were also differences in the detail of religious ritual even within the group of immigrants from a single country. The earliest Jews in America followed the Sephardic *minhag*; even when the majority of members of the earliest synagogues were Ashkenazim (after about 1730), the Sephardic pattern was maintained. In the early part of the nineteenth century, as the slow growth of Jewish population allowed, synagogues of the Ashkenazic *minhag* were founded. Later in the century, with vastly increased numbers of immigrants from each of the Eastern European countries, even local variations of pattern were made the basis for founding separate synagogues. Beyond the common ritual pattern, or *minhag,* brought from Poland, which was different from the *minhag* of Germany, there were local modifications, as of Warsaw, or of Minsk. Beyond the general Ashkenazic pronunciation of the Hebrew of the liturgy (so different from the Sephardic), there were sufficient variations among the Ashkenazic groups to make the new immigrant on the American shores feel less comfortable— perhaps even acutely uncomfortable—in a synagogue whose European roots were other than his own.

Beyond all these specifiable reasons for preferring a small congregation of comigrants from the same European *shtetl,* we must take into account the sense of "lostness." The feeling may, in many cases, have gone beyond this to what Durkheim called *anomie.* Those who came from small Eastern European villages or towns, or even from small ghetto sections of larger cities, into the vast openness of America, felt the need to huddle together for mutual comfort into small congregations, *landsmanshaften.* They identified themselves not with conceptual groups so abstract as world Jewry, or American Jewry, or New York Jewry, or even East Side Jewry, but with their *landsleit* from the *shtetl* from which they had migrated. This type of identification may have faded by now, but about fifty years ago the streets of New York were still dotted with many a little *chevra* whose name included reference to a town in Poland or Lithuania or Galicia. These small synagogues provided a kind of identification that the newcomers could feel immediately, a buffer against the new world in which, as "greenhorns," they felt so lost.

There was also a caste system within Jewry that must be reckoned with. True, it was not a rigidly ordered system, but rather its various levels were differently placed by different groups. For the Sephardim, the Sephardim occupied the top rung; for the German Jews, the favored group was the German Jews; and so on. The term "intermarriage" was used of marriages between members of two of these internal castes, as freely as it was used of marriages between Jews and non-Jews. This was still common usage long after 1880. Indeed, residues of such a caste system still persist, though now chiefly in jokes told in Jewish circles.

As a result of this type of historical background, welfare activities, through which the whole Jewish group might very well have been unified, tended instead to be duplicative and wasteful. Usually the better-established Western European Jews set up and managed a philanthropic foundation for the benefit of the newer arrivals. As soon as the newcomers had their feet on the ground, they began to resent the attitudes of patronage that such a system of welfare institutions tended to breed. So they took steps to provide for their own, and soon there were two of each kind of welfare institution. Affiliation, still with its primary meaning of belonging to a synagogue, may secondarily have meant belonging to a social or benevolent organization; but these organizations, too, though perhaps not to the same degree as the synagogues, were originally self-segregated by areas of the European roots of their members. Even B'nai B'rith was for a long time the German Jewish society. In the nineteenth century, Jews of Eastern European background were not admitted to membership; up to the early twentieth century they were still not welcomed. Only within the past forty or fifty years of American Jewish history has B'nai B'rith become an open organization. Synagogues, fraternal orders, and benevolent societies all maintained a voluntary character. Nobody forced a Jew to be a member of a synagogue, just as nobody forced him to become a member of any social or philanthropic organization.

Too often we forget that voluntaryism is a two-edged sword. It must allow for voluntary nonaffiliation as well as for voluntary affiliation. Voluntaryism cannot say one *must* affiliate with some group, but that it is a matter of indifference with which group one affiliates. Nonaffiliation must remain a live option. True, there may be some forms of group pressure that can be applied informally to encourage affiliation. Among an immigrant population, this informal pressure would be effective especially during the period of first settlement when, for various reasons, most of the new arrivals lived in close proximity. Noncoercive sanctions could be applied, but these sanctions lost their effectiveness as soon as the Jewish immigrants, finding themselves with jobs and starting to move up the ladder of success, losing their strangeness and sense of alienation from the American scene, began to scatter through the city and through the country. Once the initial phase of huddling together was past, the strongest force making for continued Jewish affiliation was discrimination in the renting of apartments and the sale of houses. The most effective unifying force was not the biblical covenant of Sinai but the restrictive covenant of real estate.

The centrifugal force of desire to get away from prying neighbors who assumed the right to police one's kitchen and one's method of child rearing as well as one's habits of synagogue attendance, was particularly strong among those who had already tasted the heady joys of secularism and socialism in Europe but who were there unable to break away because the Jewish community was still a functional reality. When they got into a situation where the community was not a reality of any sort, then they could break away if the external situation permitted. The centripetal force working to hold the Jews together was the residual anti-Semitism latent in American life. As, in any given period, American anti-Semitism loses strength, the tendency of Jews to break away from Jewish neighborhoods gains strength. Both the decrease of anti-Semitism and the increased diffusion of Jews among the population may possibly develop because of the growing Americanization of the Jew. "Look whom I brought home for dinner" may still raise a significant issue if the one who has been brought home is obviously and visibly different from his hosts. But who can tell, walking along the streets of New York City or sitting in a subway car, who are the Italian, the Jewish, the Armenian, the Greek, the Spanish, or even, in many cases, those of "pure" Anglo-Saxon stock? Is there any external and visible sign of these different forms of inner grace? One may go into Riverside Church in New York City on a Sunday and see hundreds of faces. Who can tell how many of these had Jewish ancestry? If one prefers, he can try the same experiment in Temple Emanu-El or B'nai Jeshurun or Shearith Israel and note how few of those in attendance look any different from their fellow Americans.

The Americanization process that seems to be a factor in the increase of intermarriage affects not only clothing, voice, manners, and diction. It also influences appearance, modes of thought, and attitudes toward life. Thus a non-Jewish girl could bring a Jewish boy home for dinner without anyone in the family, including the girl herself, being aware of any difference. Indeed, the prevalence among physicians, during the last couple of generations, of the

notion that there are good hygienic reasons for universal circumcision has done away with consciousness of differences even under
far less formal circumstances. Thus this Americanization process has
led to a situation in which the centrifugal force, the force leading to
a breaking away from Jewish affiliation, is much stronger than the
centripetal force holding Jews together. Just at the time when fresh
immigration ceased to be a significant factor, in the 1920s, affiliation
with synagogues, Jewish identification through synagogue membership, dropped considerably. It was at this time that the educated
guesses that pass for statistics in the Jewish field began to estimate
the total ethnically Jewish population as nearly twice the size of the
population affiliated with synagogues.

As this drop in synagogue affiliation was taking place, a new
mode of Jewish identification came to the fore. Vast numbers of
American Jews who no longer adhered to the synagogue joined with
others who retained their synagogue ties in an enthusiastic dedication to the Zionist cause. Opposition to Zionism was strong in some
Reform and some Orthodox circles, but even there the opposition
faded rapidly. The American Council for Judaism, which speaks for
the anti-Zionist position, is a small fringe group in the Reform
synagogues; the Agudah is a small fringe group in the Orthodox
synagogues. Much more characteristic of American Jewry was the
inclusiveness of Zionist enthusiasm, both in the first idealistic
thrust of the 1920s and in the soberer but no less ardent response to
Nazi anti-Semitism in the 1930s. Many Zionists also maintained
synagogue affiliation. There were also some of the unsynagogued
who became ardent Zionists. Of these it can be said that their
Jewish identification was made by support of the Zionist cause. For
a full analysis of the Zionist affiliations of unsynagogued American
Jews, it would be necessary to separate and evaluate independently
the influence of the two intermingled ideas of Homeland and
Refuge. Here we need only note that support of Zionism for either
or both of these ends provides a means consistent with the
American voluntary tradition whereby a Jewish consciousness can
be expressed without acceptance of Judaism. There is a change from
affiliation with Judaism to identification by Jewishness. Horace
Kallen has put this difference in terms of Hebraism versus Judaism.
There is need for a set of terms to express the possibility of a Jewish

identification that does not feel in any way strongly involved with synagogues. This type of ardent Zionist affiliation became less important after 1948. Zionism served as a substitute religion, and it played a very important role in American Jewish life. But by 1948 or soon thereafter it had run its course. Not that many American Jews stopped being Zionists, though some undoubtedly did, but Zionism as the focus of Jewish identification no longer commanded the same degree of emotional intensity, except possibly at moments of crisis like the Six-Day War of 1967, or the Yom Kippur War of 1973.

At about the same time that Jewish identification by affiliation with Zionism began to diminish, there was a noteworthy return to synagogue affiliation as part of the general return to church membership that the America of the 1950s heralded as a "religious revival," but that the late Rabbi Charles Shulman called a "revival without religion." Now, however, this was only one of the forms of Jewish affiliation. Other forms have been equally prevalent since the 1960s. To regard oneself, or to be regarded by others, as a Jew, even as a "good Jew," has no necessary relation to synagogue affiliation. It may have nothing to do with working with Jewish philanthropic or fraternal organizations or with contributing to Jewish causes. For many American Jews, serving the general community leads to the feeling that they are expressing their Judaism in their lives, whether or not they have any specifically Jewish affiliation. This secular and moralistic version of Jewish identification is American, very American.

A civic moral attitude has become an acceptable replacement for a religious attitude. The extent to which this shift has prevailed among Jews may be used as a measure of the Americanization of the Jew. Like other Americans, many Jews have moved from a traditional religious outlook to what John C. Bennett, former president of Union Theological Seminary, has called "culture religion." One could argue that this transition has been particularly easy for Jews because of the traditional Jewish emphasis on practice rather than doctrine. All that is necessary is to secularize and generalize the concept of *mitzva*, which has been done widely on the American Jewish scene. The Jews in America have certainly been Americanized, not always in the highest sense of that term, but it is also true and worthy of comment that American culture has been Judaized, not always in the best sense.

The Jews have become so well integrated into American life that it is no longer essential to their well-being to have a special life of their own as Jews. This being so, it is no longer necessary for an individual Jew to have a special identification as a Jew by affiliating with a synagogue. Paradoxically, however, when synagogue affiliation ceased to be necessary for the Jew as Jew, it became necessary for the Jew as American. It was part of the American mores, part of the folkways of America, especially in the post-World War II suburbs, to belong to an organization that was at least nominally religious. When Dwight Eisenhower was president of the United States, he defined an American citizen as, first, a member of a religious group, adding that it makes no difference what religious group, just so long as he belongs to a religious group. But while the necessity for manifesting this nominal religiosity has passed among other Americans, it is still strong among Jews, because of their social isolation.

Local Community or National Unity?

The small *chevra* made up of former neighbors from the same small village in Eastern Europe, as we have seen, eased the problem of alienation for the new arrival. These small, local communal congregations constituted a face-to-face primary group of people who shared a common past and a common present and looked forward to a common future. Both literally and metaphorically, the members of such a *chevra* "spoke the same language." They made up a *Gemeinschaft*, not a *Gesellschaft*. In a *chevra*, the members were an extended family that provided a natural rerooting for the deracinated Jew from Eastern Europe.

This sort of local community was by no means the goal that Isaac Leeser or Isaac M. Wise in the nineteenth century, or any of their successors in the early twentieth century, envisioned. These leaders sought to create a national unity by forging a union of congregations. They hoped to establish a national authority for American Judaism, a governing body for the Jews of the United States. It may well be that the results of their failure will ultimately be seen as disastrous for Judaism in America. Given the nature of American institutions and the variety of the Jewish population, failure was inevitable. Every attempt to achieve complete Jewish unity on a nationwide basis has failed for the same reasons. Even if there should be a religious rapprochement—a most unlikely turn of events—other factors will preclude the development of an overarching unity.

Each fragmentary group of Jews, from whatever part of the world its members or their forebears came, still cherishes, above all, its congregational independence—a trait in respect to which American and Jewish attitudes reinforce each other. The need for congregational independence had special force between 1880 and 1914 because new immigrant groups were constantly arriving in the United States. Each contingent of newcomers considered itself to be the "saving remnant" and tried to maintain its view of Judaism in spite of the pressures for modification in American Jewry. Those who had arrived earlier, or those who came from a different part of Europe with different customs, were looked upon as little better than apostates. For a few years, by isolating itself as much as possible from the corrupting influences of the environment, each little nuclear group managed to transplant its European life almost unmodified. As we have seen in chapter 2, the length of time during which this was possible depended upon the size of the group, its ability to be self-sufficient, where the members settled, what occupations they adopted, how long it took for the primary needs of life to force them out of their self-constituted ghettos into contact with the life of the host environment. Sooner or later, every group began to adjust to the American Jewish cultural scene, often without conscious awareness that it was doing so. The now not-so-new group became the target of scorn for more recent arrivals, and so the cycle was repeated.

Before 1880, when the immigrants arrived individually or in small family groups, the process of adjustment was fairly rapid. But later, when the Jewish inhabitants of a Russian or Polish town emigrated as a body, settled together in the same quarter of a large American city, maintained their own small school for their children's education and their own small synagogue, and in all ways served as a social brake on one another, adjustment came more slowly. Though it might take two generations for the process of Americanization to get its start, start it did in the end, leaving, perhaps, a handful of the oldest members of the group wondering whether they had done wrong in leaving their European home a half-century earlier.

Thus, through the local synagogue groups and whatever supplementary social groupings they bred (burial societies, societies for
visiting and aiding the sick, care for orphans, etc.), small-scale
community living remained a major force in the lives of the
immigrant Jews. Their movement into the mainstream of American
Jewish life took place by degrees, at a speed determined by the
environments from which they had come, without the emergence
of a concern for a structure of national unity. Whatever nascent
trends toward national federation had shown themselves before
1885, the new arrivals, who soon constituted a majority of the Jews
of the United States, saw no reason to work for a broader unity than
that of their own congregations. Both religiously and socially, local
community has been more central to Jewish life than national
unity.

There has been more success in federating the many Jewish
agencies in the field of welfare in all its aspects than there has been
in matters of religion. But even in philanthropy, health, or Jewish
education, despite repeated attempts, there has never developed
among American Jews, for any purpose except fund-raising, a
permanent national organization that crosses all internal lines of
division. An American Jewish communal structure, therefore,
seems destined to be no more than a Utopian dream.

A Theory of American-Jewish Community

One major attempt has been made in American-Jewish thought to
set forth a theoretical statement of the conditions of community
organization taking full cognizance of all the factors working to
prevent such an overall organization. Its author was Mordecai M.
Kaplan, founder of the Reconstructionist movement. Though the
plan is the social expression of Kaplan's broader philosophy of
Judaism, even many of those who are in total disagreement with his
theological views have given much attention and some support to
Kaplan's program for developing American Jewish communities.[6]

A major reason for the interest shown in his program is that
Kaplan sought to devise a centralized structure without sacrificing
democratic pluralism. To attain this miraculous result he formulated three basic principles. The first of these, aiming to overcome
the lack of a clear-cut definition of what is Jewish, was that all those

whose explicit purpose is to contribute to the improvement of Jewish life in America are to be welcomed as members of the planned national organization. This principle, as Kaplan has made clear in a number of supplementary statements, makes it possible to include all varieties of religiously affiliated Jews in a broad union with those many others whose understanding of "Jewish life" is exclusively ethnic or secular. It was his contention that there must be a place for the unaffiliated and the unsynagogued if the community structure is to be truly overarching.

Kaplan's second principle asserted a hierarchy of values among the different kinds of Jewish organizations. The criterion by which organizations should be judged is the centrality of their work to the heightening of Jewish consciousness. Application of this principle would invert the characteristic pattern that has emerged in American Jewish life. Instead of the welfare organizations taking the lion's share of attention and financing, in Kaplan's theory synagogues, schools, and cultural organizations would be granted priority. It is noteworthy that occasional lip service has been given to this principle in the community councils that have been established, but, despite the half-century that has passed since Kaplan's ideas were presented, the actual priorities remain much as they were then.

The third basic principle was that the existing groups engaged in specific activities shall not become merely administrative or bureaucratic arms of the community council but shall participate, in addition to their particular tasks, in the discussions of the council. In formulating this principle, Kaplan may have sought to avoid the undemocratic character that developed in many of the Jewish communities of the Old World. His total plan was to grant to each of the groups involved a virtual autonomy in all except some administrative and financial matters and a voice through its representatives in those limited areas excluded from autonomy.

An organized community then, as Kaplan envisaged it, would have a general membership, providing support for all communal activities; a democratically chosen body of representatives constituting a policy-making governing council; an administrative committee and a board of executive officers charged with the duty of implementing the decisions of the council and supervising the execution of the council's policies; some "functional bureaus" under the control of the council, organized to carry out the everyday activities of the community; and, finally, those other groups organized for "specific Jewish purposes" whose virtual autonomy and participation in policy making was the subject of the third principle. Kaplan's design was not a Jewish communal structure on what is popularly thought to be the lines of the New England "town meeting," where every voice was to be given equal weight. His purpose was, rather, to suggest a way in which "every Jewish interest or tendency which is manifest in the community" can be taken account of in the planning of communal policy.

This theory, which tries to reclaim the positive values of the traditional European Jewish community by a deliberate reconstruction along lines more suitable to the American Jewish group, has been criticized on a number of counts. In general, those who look at it from the perspective of professional workers in the welfare aspects of Jewish life are not pleased that cultural and synagogal activities are ranked as more centrally relevant to Jewish consciousness raising than their own activities. From the standpoint of synagogue leaders, the plan allows the unsynagogued, "secular" Jews too large a role in policy. Only in the context of the Reconstructionist position, which Kaplan himself has done most to define, does the plan make sense as a totality.

Then, too, America's Jews are as resistant as other Americans to the notion of rationally planned, consistently ordered societal schemes, whether in political or in religious affairs. Ad hoc voluntary associations across denominational lines do occur today and have occurred from time to time in American Judaism. A few instances of permanent cooperation for limited ends have been established. For the most part, however, congregational independence remains the prevalent mode of organized Jewish life. Indeed congregationalism is so dominant that even the "denominations" are more accurately described as federations, since they lack any authority to compel conformity to their decisions.

The Synagogue-Center

Because the notion of centralized control in any form whatsoever is anathema to the vast majority of the Jews of the United States, the synagogue has become the most characteristic and distinctive form of Jewish organization. The synagogue is not only the focus of religious life in its three traditional forms—study (*torah*), worship (*abodah*), and philanthropy (*gemilut hasadim*)—but also the social center for its members and their families. In this respect, even though American Jews are largely residents of urban and suburban areas, their synagogues resemble the Protestant churches of rural Christianity in America.

To list even a few of the varied activities carried on within the synagogues of the United States makes clear the centrality of the relatively small congregational unit to Jewish life. The very shape of newer synagogue buildings reinforces the impact of such a listing. The basic worship services on the Sabbath and holidays remain the core of synagogal activity and are housed in a segment of the building known as the "sanctuary." Often, especially in urban synagogues where space is at a premium, the sanctuary per se is a comparatively small area backed by folding doors that conceal an all-purpose area. When the doors are open, this space forms part of an enlarged sanctuary for those services at which larger attendance may be anticipated. At other times, the all-purpose room may be used for a wide range of other activities of a secular cast without the use being offensive to anyone, as it might well be if the area were a permanent part of the sanctuary. In some synagogues there is also a smaller sanctified room, or chapel, where daily morning and evening prayer services may be held, or weddings for small parties, or funeral services with few mourners.

Second in importance to worship in the American synagogue is the commandment of study. This is fulfilled in many ways on many levels, often under the direct leadership of a junior or assistant rabbi. The education of the children of the congregation may be pursued exclusively through a Sunday school, or through a combination of Sunday and one, two, or three weekday afternoon sessions, or, in an increasing number of instances, through congregationally maintained "all-day" schools, teaching all the standard materials of a secular school curriculum and "religious" studies as well. The earliest Jewish Sunday schools in the United States were started in Philadelphia by Rebecca Gratz and Isaac Leeser in direct and deliberate imitation of Protestant Sunday schools. Leeser wrote (or adapted from German originals) textbook materials for these schools. In the twentieth century, each of the major denominations has developed a cadre of educational professionals who create both curricular and co-curricular materials which are then made available to the synagogues for use in their schools. Each of the rabbinical seminaries offers potential rabbis some training in educational theory so that they can become supervisors of the formal schooling process in their congregations. There are special schools for the training of teachers for these congregational schools.

The synagogues do not neglect the education of the adult members of the congregation, although it is seldom as systematically organized as the education of the youth. For the most part, adult education is limited to lecture programs with some opportunity for discussion. In Orthodox synagogues one may find a small group meeting on Sabbath afternoons for intensive study of the Talmud. This type of traditional study group (*chevra shas*) is less likely to develop in a Conservative or Reform congregation, but a similar voluntary group may read together in a major work of Jewish philosophy or mysticism under the guidance of the rabbi. On the whole, the synagogues fulfill their educational responsibilities to their members reasonably well.

With regard to the third of the primary obligations, philanthropy or, more precisely, deeds of loving-kindness, the synagogues today are less immediately involved. The professionalization of philanthropic activities and the emergence of the specialized organizations of social work and their attendant bureaucracies have, for better or worse, reduced the participation of the synagogue and its membership very largely to a conduit for funds to be expended outside of the congregation. There may be a local need to be met—for example, a hospital—but again, once the fund-raising has been done, the professionals dominate.

On the social side, activities that take place in the synagogue tend to increase exponentially. Groups for men or for women, for couples, for particular ages, for specific interests, for any purpose that arises within the congregation, flourish and proliferate. Troops of Boy Scouts or Girl Scouts may use synagogue facilities. Many synagogues have gymnasiums and swimming pools, and some field their own athletic teams. So full is the program that scheduling and traffic control can themselves become administrative problems.

From the synagogue as one agency in the Jewish community, American Judaism, first unconsciously and then deliberately,
evolved the idea of the synagogue as the community center. When
Mordecai Kaplan first explicitly formulated the concept of the
synagogue-center in 1918, he surely thought of it as a way of healing
the breach between the ethnic ideal of "Jewishness" and the
religious ideal of Judaism. There can be no doubt that the
synagogue-center has done this to some extent. In the view of many
religious leaders, however, it has led to the takeover of the
synagogue by secular interests. Rabbi Israel Goldstein has said,
"Whereas the hope of the Synagogue Center was to Synagogize the
tone of the secular activities of the family, the effect has been the
secularization of the place of the Synagogue." The most telling
comment is that of Rabbi David Aronson: "A community that
accepts the philosophy that a gymnasium is as essential to Jewish life
as a synagogue, and a Jewish basketball team as conducive to Jewish
survival as a Talmud Torah, is on its way to Jewish extinction."[7]
Kaplan himself and most spokesmen for the welfare groups have
spoken far more enthusiastically than these religious leaders of the
effect of the synagogue-center on Jewish life.[8]

As more and more new synagogues are built, it has become clear
that the synagogue-center idea has captured the imagination of the
Jewish laity. And in America what the laity like and want (and are
ready to pay for) is what the rabbis must learn to live with. One
noble-souled rabbi spoke privately of his new multimillion dollar
synagogue-center as "my gilded cage," but he sang there bril-
liantly despite his reservations about the conspicuous display the
architects had introduced in order to satisfy the dominant laity. At
the very least, the synagogue-center has not been permitted to lapse
into a merely secular center or ethnic social club, but has kept its
role as synagogue in the forefront of its concern.

6 Jew and Non-Jew: The Problem of Pluralism

The Jew as Paradigm of Cultural Pluralism

The medieval image of the Jew as the minion of Satan persisted long in the popular imagination.[1] The Jews were strangers, aliens, objects of curiosity even in the United States. Joseph Jonas, a silversmith and watchmaker from Plymouth, England, was an early settler in Cincinnati, arriving in 1817. The following year, an old Quaker lady ordered Jonas to stand still; she gave him a very thorough and searching inspection, front and back, head to toe, and then delivered herself of the remark, "Thee is no different from other people." Even in the twentieth century there are many Americans to whom a Jew is still a curious object. Jewish freshmen at colleges and universities often find themselves the focus of close attention by some fellow freshmen, especially from rural areas, who "have never seen a Jew."[2]

That Jews can still remain oddities on the American rural scene may be attributed to the fact that they have never constituted a large minority in American life and that they have tended to live in urban (and, more recently, suburban) areas. At the time of the American Revolution twenty-five hundred to three thousand Jews constituted no more than 1 percent of the total population. By 1880 there may have been as many as a quarter of a million Jews in the entire country, amounting to a bit more than 2 percent of the whole number of Americans at that time. The period between 1881 and 1914, during which many timorous Americans (including American Jews) feared that the country was being inundated by

East European Jews, ended with a Jewish population of about three and a half million out of a total population of over one hundred million, or just short of 3 ½ percent. Now, in the mid-1970s, a good guess would be that Jews still constitute less than 5 percent of the American people.

With the cutting off of mass immigration and a current tendency among Jews to a slightly lower birth rate than that of the population as a whole, the probability is that the Jewish minority will never be greater than 5 percent. Nevertheless, Will Herberg's penetrating analysis of the American scene as a "three faith" system holds true not only for the twentieth century, on which his formulation was based, but also for earlier periods, though perhaps less formally and explicitly.[3] It would be pleasant to believe that the concern for this small minority is based on a general spirit of tolerance and goodwill, as exemplified by the provision of a table of *kosher* refreshments at the conclusion of the parade celebrating the adoption of the new Constitution of the United States, in Philadelphia, in 1789. Even if it is not based on goodwill but on cold calculation of Jewish voting strength, it is a fact that the small group of American Jews is counted as on a par with the enormous Protestant and Catholic groups in matters of public policy.

In part, this special treatment is a consequence of the mobility and adaptability of the Jews of America. No other immigrant group in America's history has risen from abject poverty into the middle class as rapidly or as completely as the East European Jews of the 1880-1914 immigration. No other group has become enculturated with American middle-class values and ideals as rapidly or as completely. Many other groups can point to large numbers of individual achievers; what is notable in the Jewish instance is the phenomenally rapid rise to middle-class status of an entire group. There is fairly responsible and adequate scientific knowledge that the gene pool for all peoples is roughly equal. It would be naïve, on the basis of present information, to account for the rapid rise of the Jews by any assertion of an innate superiority of an entire people. Jewish upward mobility cannot be caused by any elements in their genetic nature; the causes must be sought in the elements of Jewish nurture. Three such elements stand out.

First, as has been pointed out frequently, the middle-class ethos, its characteristic patterns of goals and values, especially as it has manifested itself in the United States of America, is largely derived from the Calvinist tradition of Protestant Christianity. The value system that the immigrant Jews brought with them is so similar to the Calvinist pattern, both being grounded in a nomistic, if not a legalistic, interpretation of the Old Testament, that acceptance of American middle-class values presented no problems. Long before they had risen into the middle class, the Jews adhered to what, in the United States at least, were decidedly middle-class attitudes. Hard work, thrift, readiness to defer satisfaction in the present for the sake of goals to be achieved in the future, temperance in personal habits, even an intense feeling for social respectability (sometimes only for the outward signs of social respectability)— these are attitudes and values common to the Protestant American middle class and to the Jews even as immigrants trying to scratch out a bare living.

Second, among the immigrant Jews there was a strong sense of family that produced innumerable instances of mutual assistance.[4] In part, this may derive from the age-old Jewish tradition that it would be a scandal if any one of their number was forced to ask and accept assistance from the non-Jewish public. It was a matter of pride to the Jewish community that it took care of its own. Philanthropy ranks very high in Jewish ethics; the details are spelled out in practical terms in the rabbinic codes. In part, too, the strong loyalties within the extended family may have been produced by the centuries of living in hostile environments where the solidarity of the kinship group was one of the few resources on which the Jewish individual could rely. The family was a source of mutual aid for its members not only in times of adversity, but even in times of prosperity. Any Jew who moved ahead saw to it that he carried others with him, as far as it was possible for him to do so.

In the United States, where the general openness of the economic scene did not remind the Jews incessantly of the need to help each other, and where, thanks to the public schools, the Americanization of the young proceeded far more rapidly than that of their elders, it was common in all new American groups, Jewish or not, for a deep generation gap to develop. The older sense of family was basically challenged by the embarrassment and even shame that the

Americanized young felt for their still European relatives. The burden of holding the immigrant family together despite generational differences fell most heavily to one member—the mother. It is the Jewish mother who has been most often, and most mordantly, portrayed in the literature. But the same traits that have made the Jewish mother a byword and a stock character in twentieth-century American literature were manifested by other immigrant mothers. That it has been so largely the Jewish mother who appears in the literature is a consequence of her success as well as of the probably temporary prominence of Jews in the literary world.

The prominence of Jews in literature and in other aspects of the high cultural scene suggests a third element in Jewish nurture that profoundly affected their social mobility. From ancient times, study, conceived as study of Torah, has been considered one of the three pillars upon which the religious life was based. The tradition of Judaism regarded study as the most proper vocation of man; his occupation, the way in which he earned his living, was secondary to his study. In Western Europe toward the late eighteenth century and in Eastern Europe somewhat later, the traditional conception of study became secularized. The study of Torah was still most highly prized, but other studies in all forms of modern knowledge and skills were almost as highly regarded. In the United States, possibly because of the immediate utility of modern secular studies in making one's place in the world secure, the order of priority came to be reversed. Scholastic achievement in the public elementary schools, distinction in the work of the high schools, admission to college, the winning of scholarships, prizes, and awards, admission to a professional school, all leading to a secure and respectable place in society as a doctor, a dentist, a lawyer, an accountant, a teacher—this was the kind of vision each Jewish family had for its young male hopefuls.[5]

That families should have such dreams is not particularly Jewish, certainly not exclusively Jewish. Every family of whatever background envisions a brighter future for the new generation. What is outstanding is the sacrifice that all members of the Jewish immigrant family were willing to make to advance those who showed potential for fulfilling the vision. Noteworthy is the extent to which those who did scale the heights—having benefited from their family's sacrifice—used their achievements and their prominence to ease the lives of those who had supported and encouraged them. After all, the rarest of human virtues is gratitude, and still rarer is gratitude expressed in tangible ways. What is most remarkable is the docility with which the Jewish youths accepted the roles their elders had dreamed for them, studied harder, applied themselves, minimized their social lives, so largely avoided the usual collegiate experimentation with various forms of distraction and dissipation that an unusually large proportion of them did attain and even surpass their parents' imaginings.

As a result, many of the younger members of even the immigrant generation rose into the middle class, a far larger number of the second generation, and virtually all of the third generation. So recent was this transformation of a penniless immigrant group escaping persecution into an affluent, economically and professionally secure middle class, that the young people now in college are, at most, a fourth generation. In this generation some change of outlook has become evident. The highly competitive, achievement-oriented spirit that carried the previous generation so far, so fast, is apparently being rejected wholesale by the rising generation. Where, in earlier times, the generation gap among the Jewish group took relatively minor forms—quarrels over the use of English rather than Yiddish, unwillingness to devote a sufficiently large proportion of study time to the Jewish tradition, modernization of home decor or of modes of dress—today the gap is at the very center. For a substantial segment of Jewish fourth-generation youth has rejected the ethos of the earlier generations: hard work, thrift, the readiness to defer satisfaction in the present for the sake of goals to be achieved, the intense desire for social respectability or, at the least, its outward signs.

Other members of the fourth generation reveal clear evidences of what Robert Redfield called "contra-acculturation." As Redfield defined this counterprocess, it involves a deliberate attempt to retain an older cultural heritage, partly as a compensation for inferior status and partly as a badge of distinction to gain prestige in one's own group. It should be added that much of the apparent "orthodoxy" of contra-acculturated American Jewish youth involves a distrust of the sincerity of American society and a deliberate testing of American pretensions. These young people seem to be saying to their neighbors: "All right; you claim that this is an open, prejudice-free society. Maybe it is; maybe it isn't. Let's see just how far this openness goes and how long it lasts when it is confronted with a visible badge of difference."

Anti-Semitism and the Jewish Response

The flaunting of difference, for whatever reason, carried on by part of the Jewish group is the result of an awareness bred into even the most prestigious of America's Jews that anti-Semitic attitudes lie very close to the surface of American life. Despite the absence of legal restrictions, restrictiveness crops up in many phases of life. Thomas Jefferson himself, in most respects a shining example of open-mindedness and tolerance, once wrote to a Jewish correspondent that, though he supported political equality for Jews, he did not like them. More recently many non-Jews have been shocked to find evidence of anti-Semitism in the transcribed tapes of Richard Nixon's conversation with his aides; few Jews were surprised.

One result of the ever-present undercurrent of anti-Jewish attitudes has been the development in the United States of a number of organizations devoted with religious fervor to Jewish self-defense, on a variety of fronts. There are some organizations, like the American Jewish Committee, that adopt a quasi-ambassadorial stance as representatives of the Jewish people to the government of the United States and to other governments around the world. At the opposite extreme are the semi-underground guerrillas of the Jewish Defense League. In between, attempting chiefly to educate the non-Jewish public, are such groups as the Anti-Defamation League of B'nai B'rith. The prevalence of such organizations shows how far, even under the pluralistic conditions of life in the United States, Jews feel insecure. Jewish history justifies their sense of insecurity. Some of the worst anti-Semitic persecutions and pogroms, up to and including the Holocaust of the twentieth century, occurred in countries of the world where the Jews felt most firmly a part of the life of their host country. The Jewish defense organizations in the United States manifest a tacit agreement that when (not if) "it" happens here, "we" will not be unprepared.

To some extent the constant concern with what is called "maintaining Jewish identity" is a closely related phenomenon of American Jewish life. A small minority, without physical distinction from the majority, increasingly like the majority in language, behavioral traits, education, range of occupational distribution, and other matters making up the complex called "culture," can easily disappear into that majority, losing the last remaining shreds of differentiation. The preservation of Judaism, the last difference, is essential to the survival of the Jews of America. Paradoxically, however, the preservation of the Jewish people as an ethnic minority within the culturally plural setting of the United States is essential to the perpetuation of Judaism within the religiously plural setting of the United States. In ultimate terms, Judaism and Jewishness support and maintain each other.

Ultimately, then, the frequently challenged activities of the "religious" organizations in sponsoring study of conversational Hebrew, group tours to Israel, Jewish troops of Boy Scouts, Girl Scouts, or Campfire Girls, and other such expressions of secular Jewishness do contribute importantly to maintaining Judaism. Moreover, the often denigrated activities of Jewish fraternal organizations in providing ties holding Jews together in primarily social bonds—even by means that many religious leaders resent, such as Little League baseball teams—also help to sustain Judaism.

Most visibly, B'nai B'rith, through its Hillel Foundation, has done yeoman service in preserving the loyalties of the Jewish youth through the active Hillel societies in many of the colleges and universities of the country. B'nai B'rith is not alone in this work; other organizations now contribute meaningfully, with other special publics. The Jewish War Veterans is one such. The mainly (indeed, overwhelmingly) Jewish membership of certain fraternities and sororities in colleges and high schools across the nation provides other examples. The roster of organizations of a primarily social character in any community with a sizable Jewish population yields others.

It is idle to argue whether social activities and the spiritual life ought to be in such close connection. The philosopher or the psychologist, the theologian or the clergyman, may argue endlessly about the need that all men have for a distinct spiritual life, for a clear line of demarcation between the sacred and profane aspects of life. It is dubious, at best, whether this need is felt by people in modern times. For most people, day-to-day social contact with their fellow humans probably provides sufficient spiritual uplift and opportunity for self-transcendence. The life of fraternal and sororal organizations is extremely satisfying in these regards because it is enhanced by a modicum of exclusiveness and presumed secrecy, accompanied by an attractively designed ritual. From the days before the American Revolution to our own times the fraternal and sororal orders have provided for some a supplement and for others a substitute for synagogue activities. They have differed in the degree to which the preservation of Judaism was their explicit concern, but they have, willy-nilly, helped to preserve Judaism.[6]

In their earliest days in the United States, Jews were attracted to Scottish Rite Freemasonry, perhaps because of its universalistic conception of fraternity. Moses M. Hays of New York and Boston is actually credited with having introduced the Scottish Rite into the American colonies. In 1768, he was appointed Deputy Inspector General of Masonry for North America, and was himself responsible for appointing other Jews to high posts in Masonic circles.[7] Hays was Master of King David's Lodge in New York City, founded 17 February 1769. "This Lodge appears to have been composed entirely of Jewish Brethren."[8] Later, about 1779, this all-Jewish lodge moved to Newport, Rhode Island. Moses Seixas, one of the leaders of the then large Jewish community of Newport, served as Grand Master of the Grand Lodge of Rhode Island. Jews have continued to be active as Masons until the present. Increasingly, especially in the larger communities, all-Jewish lodges have been established, with rabbis who are Masons serving as chaplains and celebrating the fraternal rituals. Despite its original appeal to a universal brotherhood, Masonry has in practice become a semisegregated fraternity.

In 1843, a new departure in Jewish organizational behavior in the United States was made when a group of the leading German Jewish citizens of New York City founded the Independent Order of B'nai B'rith. From this time on, although Jews continued to belong to Masonic lodges, Jewish activity in fraternal orders was increasingly in the Jewish orders. In addition to elements of ritual and organization that paralleled those of the Masons, B'nai B'rith and the other Jewish orders took over some of the functions formerly exercised by burial societies and mutual aid groups among the Jews. Until the twentieth century, the membership of B'nai B'rith was largely homogeneous. Even in its early days, however, it occasionally welcomed into its fellowship those of non-German background. As the order spread widely and rapidly in the Jewish population centers outside of New York City, this unofficial limitation was no longer maintained. Over the years, most of the secret ritual of B'nai B'rith has been abandoned, more democratic control has been fostered in the order, and a wide variety of worthwhile programs, including the Hillel Foundation and the Anti-Defamation League, developed. Soon after B'nai B'rith was founded, other Jewish fraternal organizations followed: the Independent Order of Free Sons of Israel (1849), B'rith Abraham (1859), Kesher shel Barzel (1860). Later these were supplemented by others, including a major sororal organization, the United Order of True Sisters. The later Eastern European immigrants felt a need for like organizations, especially of a working-class orientation. They brought into being the Workmen's Circle and the Jewish National Workers Alliance.

It is interesting to note that B'nai B'rith originally intended to "banish from its deliberations all doctrinal and dogmatic discussion and by the practice of moral and benevolent precepts bring about union and harmony."[9] Thus, by the very terms of its foundation, those who chose to identify themselves as Jews solely by morality and benevolence and to allow their ceremonial and ritual practice and their synagogue affiliations to lapse could build a moralistic Judaism through the work of B'nai B'rith. A non-Jewish writer in 1871 envisioned B'nai B'rith as an agency for the complete transformation of Judaism into a social service activism: "The order of B'nai B'rith, the Sons of the Covenant, is to the Jewish Church what the Christian associations are to the Christian Church, a liberalizing influence, as it turns the people from forms and rites and from speculative questions to work of practical reform and charity."[10] The order may have done this for some of its members and may still do so. For most members of B'nai B'rith and the other fraternal orders, the organizations serve a merely social function. But there are others whose total Jewish consciousness is expressed in their fraternal membership, and for this reason the orders must be

ranked among the agencies of the spiritual life of the Jews of the
United States.

The Social World of the Jew in America

Periodically the American Jews find their ease in the United States
threatened by Christian missionary activity as well as by anti-
Semitism. For the most part, Jewish fear of Christian missions is
highly, if understandably, exaggerated. A people whose history
records many enforced conversions in both Muslim and Christian
lands is unlikely to take a light view of any attempt at conversion,
however scant the force behind it may be. Many Jews believe that
any approach Christians make to a social relation with Jews has
overtones of conversion. Quite obviously this fear is not justified in
most instances, any more than is the fear some Christians have of
world Jewish conspiracies. Nevertheless, it constitutes an important
barrier between Jews and Christians because what is important in
the lives of people is rarely what is true but is, rather, what is
believed to be true.

Partly, then, because the Jews in general fear too much social
contact, and partly because many non-Jews in America prefer to live
a social life that is *Judenrein,* and despite ecumenical spirits and the
efforts of such high-level organizations as the National Conference
of Christians and Jews, the American Jew still lives in a social
ghetto. He may, and indeed most often does, work in an open and
pluralistic economic order, where not his religious or ethnic
background but his capacity to do his job well is the criterion of his
acceptance. Socially, however, his day is divided, even as is the day
of the American Black, by what is cynically referred to in both
groups as "five o'clock shadow." Whatever intimacy the Jewish
person may maintain through the day with non-Jewish coworkers
ends, as a general rule, when the shop or office closes. By tacit
mutual agreement the Jew is not part of the social world of his or
her non-Jewish fellow workers, nor do they enter the Jew's social
world. If the Jew does have, or must have because of his position,
social contact with coworkers outside of business hours, the occasion
is likely to be a formal one. It is not an informal or casual social
mixing of people but a carefully planned gathering, to which, one

often finds, all the Jews who for one reason or another must be invited are invited in a bloc.

This arrangement is, again for the most part, supported by the manner of American living. For all the laws on the statute books banning discrimination in the sale or rental of living accommodations, Jews, by and large, live still in "Jewish" neighborhoods, as Irish live in "Irish" neighborhoods, and Italians in "Italian" neighborhoods. Some of the enormously expensive cooperative apartment buildings in fashionable areas of New York City have Jewish owners only. These are ghettos, even though platinum ghettos set with diamonds. Some suburban housing developments are owned almost entirely by Jews. And, of course, other cooperative apartment buildings and suburban housing developments have gentle—and sometimes not so gentle—ways of discouraging Jewish purchasers.

Socially, then, the Jew in America lives as other Americans of the same educational and income stratum live, but overwhelmingly he does all that he does outside of working hours with other Jews, not with non-Jews. If he joins a country club, it is a Jewish country club; if he plays golf or bridge, or if he bowls, it is most often in the company of other Jews; if his tastes run to attendance at plays, concerts, or dance recitals, his companions, those with whom he shares his recreations and his reactions, are in most instances his fellow Jews. In this respect, the twentieth-century Jewish experience in the United States parallels not only the Black, the Chicano, the Puerto Rican, the Italian, the Polish, the Irish experience; it parallels, too, the experience of the white, Anglo-Saxon Protestant. The United States is, as has been said, not one nation, but "a nation of nations." It is not to be wondered at, when there is so little social contact, that there is so little understanding among the various nations. No wonder that ancient myths persist. Members of each nation are, in some fashion, "curiosities" to members of other nations. If some non-Jews still believe some of the medieval legends about the Jews—that they have horns and tails and are allies of Satan, for example—many Jews grow up with comparable medieval superstitions about non-Jews.

There are some obviously unfortunate aspects to the situation as presented here, but it is not altogether bad. Insofar as a true cultural pluralism requires that the many cultures of the American scene remain vital, it also demands the preservation of differences. It is good for our plural culture that the social integrity of the Jews should not disappear in the "melting pot." It is good, too, for Judaism that in other than religious matters there should be a recognizable difference between Jews and non-Jews. There must, after all, be Jews if Judaism is to be America's "third faith," as there must be Jews if the four-thousand-year-old Jewish culture is to continue as an organically sound, developing ingredient in the American pluriculture. To the extent that social separation (*not* segregation) guarantees that all the alternative forms of twentieth-century Judaism remain as viable religious interpretations of modern Jewish life in the United States, separation is good for the Jews and for the non-Jews as well.

A true cultural pluralism requires that each cultural group must learn to respect the other cultures as well as take pride in its own unique qualities. Cultural pluralism does not imply each cultural pattern flourishing on its own. It implies, rather, that through the interplay and interaction of the various cultures, there should be an enrichment and a deepening of each separate culture, leading to an ennoblement of the cultural heritage of all. This work cannot be left entirely in the hands of writers and artists, so much of whose work in the last generation has contributed to the phenomenon that has been called the Judaizing of American culture. It must be the concern of all. It is proper for Jews as Jews to be concerned for the continuation of Jewish culture. It is no less appropriate for American Jews and their non-Jewish neighbors to be concerned as Americans for the enrichment of the American pluriculture.

The Quest for Interfaith Understanding

In nineteenth-century American synagogues, elimination of the "Oriental" elements in public worship was urged in part because non-Jews were fairly frequent attendants. Nor did Jews, as so many do today, consciously and deliberately avoid attendance at Christian religious services. The carrying on of social life in parallel lines, never meeting, that is so common in the twentieth century had not yet infected the American scene. In the smaller population and closer neighborliness of an early age there was a better basis for mutual understanding. Perhaps, too, the mere fact that both Jews and non-Jews had a familiarity with the Old Testament text created a pool of shared allusions and common terms of sacred reference and thus helped to build bridges despite differences in theological interpretations.

This community of reference to the Old Testament no longer exists for the average Jew or non-Jew. The minister, the priest, and the rabbi are familiar with the text of the shared Bible; they also share the problems of religious professionals in an age of minimal devoutness. Among these religious leaders and the small number of the laity who share the knowledge of the professionals, a move toward interfaith understanding has been slowly developing during the past half-century. This move is not a movement; it is not "ecumenical." Especially it is not an attempt to water down the distinctions between the faiths, but rather an attempt to understand how and why these distinctions have come to be. The effort is to sharpen and clarify distinctions, to make them intelligible in the light of the differing historical experiences of the faith communities involved.

Since about 1920, some rabbis, in Reform and Conservative circles especially, have participated in this slowly growing concern for mutual understanding, or have, at least, cautiously welcomed it as a device for eliminating mutual misunderstanding. Orthodox rabbis have been much more reserved about entering into interfaith discussions with non-Jews. Only during the last decade has Orthodoxy begun to waver slightly in its opposition. In 1966, one of the most highly respected of modern Orthodox leaders, Joseph I. Soloveitchik,[11] issued through the Rabbinical Council of America a statement of guidelines for interfaith dialogues. In his statement, Rabbi Soloveitchik permitted interfaith discussion on cultural and humanitarian themes, but said explicitly, "We are opposed to every public debate, dialogue or symposium concerning the doctrinal, dogmatic or ritual aspects of our faith vis-à-vis similar aspects of another faith community."[12] He listed four specific topics as "improper" for public discussion by Orthodox Jews: Jewish monotheism and the Christian idea of the Trinity, the Messianic idea in Judaism and Christianity, the Jewish view of

Jesus, and the concept of the Covenant in Judaism and Christianity. If all Orthodox Jews accepted these limitations, opportunities for fruitful dialogue at those points where understanding is most needed would be greatly diminished.

The possibility of interfaith dialogue without the intrusion of rancor may itself be considered a product of the modern mind. The medieval "disputations" had conversion, not understanding, as their object; the *odium theologicum* that prevailed was inevitably involved in the sponsorship and purpose of the public debates. Soloveitchik's guidelines presuppose the same underlying purpose and the same medieval attitude. Certainly he is correct in his estimate of the historical experience of such debates in an earlier world, although there are those even in the Orthodox camp who would not agree that there has been no change in modern times. There are no beliefs that are held more firmly than those of religion, and earlier debates offer little precedent to support advocates of interfaith discussion.

The new form of discussion demands a new attitude. Interfaith talk requires that however true each participant is to his own beliefs, he recognize the equal right of every other participant to be true to his own beliefs.[13] Interfaith discussion demands that however firmly we adhere to our own beliefs, there must be some corner of our minds that heeds the possibility that others, too, have fractional insight into the truth, even as we have. We hold the beliefs that by upbringing or conviction or a combination of the two we feel to be most probable; others, too, do the same. Our best hope must be that our beliefs are pointers toward the full truth that we can know only partially. Our religions, to the extent that they have genuinely entered into modern ways of thinking, must inevitably achieve the paradoxical position of accepting religious doctrines both totally and tentatively, for without total acceptance there can be no true commitment and without tentativeness there can be no true modernity. In the tentativeness of religious acceptance lies the hope of fruitful interfaith discussion; in the totality of the religious commitment lies the subject of discussion.

Undoubtedly there will be some leaders, in each of the faith communities, who reject the interfaith thrust of modern American religion. For the matter of that, there are Orthodox Jews who will

not enter into dialogue with Conservative or Reform Jews, funda-
mentalist Protestants who will not participate with other Protestants
in the World Council of Churches, traditionalist Catholics who
have held no communication with their fellow Catholics since the
Second Vatican Council. The obligation of the new spirit of
understanding is to attempt to understand even such rejections of
the new spirit.

The more important difficulty is that the interfaith temper is
manifested almost entirely on the level of theologians, isolated
clergymen, religious scholars, and highly informed laymen. It has
barely begun to seep down into the pulpits of the run-of-the-mill
clergy and into the congregational pews. There is scarcely a trace to
be found in the classrooms of religious elementary schools. It may
take several generations to eliminate statements of bias, partial
truths, even incitements to hate from the printed textbooks, and
the books are still more readily controlled than the casual words of
teachers.

Studies made at St. Louis University have shown that many of the
elementary textbooks used in Roman Catholic parochial schools
contain anti-Semitic statements. Undoubtedly the Reformation
and its leading figures are treated very differently in Protestant
and Catholic texts. The histories studied by Jewish children report
the Crusades in far different terms than do the texts studied by
Catholic—perhaps even by Protestant—pupils. The Inquisition,
the Religious Wars, the St. Bartholomew's Day Massacre—one
event after another in the history of the world, especially since the
sixteenth century, reads differently in the books of different faiths.
The martyrs of one community are the heretics of another. The
opportunities for imbibing prejudice are greatest in the very same
years in which children's minds are most malleable and simple
formulations most necessary. Corrections and modifications that
may come at a later stage of education may often erase the conscious
misinformation while leaving the unconscious attitudes of antagonism, hostility, and prejudice untouched. Interfaith understanding
will not come easily, even in modern America.

For all this, interfaith activity is one of the more promising ways
to bring into being the ideal America of cultural pluralism
described by Kallen as ''an orchestration of diverse utterances of

diversities—regional, local, religious, ethnic, esthetic, industrial, sporting and political—each developing freely and characteristically in its own enclave, and somehow so intertwined with the others, as to suggest, even to symbolize, the dynamic of the whole. Each is a cultural reservoir whence flows its own singularity to unite in the concrete inter-cultural total which is the culture of America."[14] There is no quick and easy way to achieve the ideal set forth here; interfaith understanding is no less in need of long-range strategies than is interracial accord. If we foolishly hope for a major change in a few short years or by executive order, disappointment is sure to come. Patience and endless concern are necessary if the readiness to understand others is ever to be carried down from the sphere of the scholar and theologian to the very texts in which the youngest children learn their religious ABC's. The problem of pluralism can be resolved, in the long run, by maintaining where it exists, and promoting where it does not, a double commitment—to one's own tradition and culture, and to the right of others to be equally committed to their own tradition and culture.

7   *The Americanization of American Judaism*

American Roots for the Uprooted

The question that has most often been asked by scholars is how the Jews living in the United States of America have become more and more like the other residents; that is, how the Jews of America have become Americanized. Other students have examined the Jewish community in the United States and questioned whether it has not become a variety of American community rather than a continued example of what the earlier European Jewish communities were like. Still others have been concerned with the psychological transition from identifying oneself as a Jew living in America to self-identification as an American Jew, and, in a second step, from American Jew to Jewish American. Only incidentally, in discussions of these matters, has the question central to this essay been touched upon. The primary concern here has been to determine how, and how extensively, the patterns of religious practice and belief of the Jews of the United States and the institutions through which these practices and beliefs are expressed have been modified by the cultural, and especially the religious, environment surrounding Judaism in America.

Heinz Politzer, a student of comic strips, wrote an essay some years ago under the title "From Little Nemo to Li'l Abner," that expressed very lucidly, in terms of the popular culture medium of his study, a theme that is most helpful to the understanding of the popular culture medium of religion:

It is here that Abie the Agent comes in. Abie Kabibble is as Jewish as the Katzenjammers are German: in him the ethnic minority enriches the American scene by the peculiarity of its speech, mentality, and group character. Abie is a *schlemiel* and a realist, outrageously sentimental and stubbornly matter-of-fact, the wandering Jew taking a short rest in the suburbs of the world. But the suburbs are those of pre-World War I America. Abie shows neither complacency nor self-hatred; his flat feet have plodded into reality and there he has settled down. He is the general underdog, proclaiming the philosophy of the socially underprivileged. He, too, is the last, the best of all the game. In his mouth, to be sure, this assurance has a faintly ironic ring.

Parenthetically, in the light of this paragraph, it is easy to understand that it is not altogether accidental that it was a Jew, Arthur Miller, who wrote *Death of a Salesman,* although Willy Loman is not presented as a Jewish character. To continue with Heinz Politzer:

Abie the Agent is the explicit contribution of American Jewry to the comic strip. Elsewhere, Jews function more as a leaven and a seasoning. Such artists as Rube Goldberg season the general trends with their wit rather than reflect themselves. And with Alfred Gerald Caplin who is Al Capp, American Jewry demonstrates its advanced position in American society. Al Capp has only to express in his strip his own desires, drives and anxieties—like, say, Saul Steinberg in his cartoons—in order to answer the desires, drives, and anxieties of all his contemporaries, regardless of variety of origin or creed. By their very name, Abie and Li'l Abner show the stages in the path American Jews have followed in integrating themselves in the context of American civilization.[1]

The point of Politzer's keen analysis is that, between the years before World War I and the present, the image of the Jew and of his role in American society changed from that of the outsider, "taking a short rest in the suburbs of the world," to that of the paradigm of American sensitivities. Within the past three-quarters of a century, approximately, Jews began to feel comfortable and at home in the United States of America and therefore to express and reflect current forms of American "consciousness." Implied, too, in what Politzer says about Al Capp is the conclusion that a large part of the non-Jewish population of the United States has begun to feel more comfortable with its Jewish neighbors, and therefore to accept this reflection of its own consciousness.

Politzer's fascinating text contains a large measure of truth, particularly with respect to the post-1881 Jewish immigration from Eastern Europe. More important, the text suggests a way of describing, if not defining, the meaning of the difficult term "Americanization." The usual method of conceptualizing this term has been to make efforts to discover objective and preferably quantifiable data by means of which to create a device for measuring Americanization. Some of the questions asked had to do with official attitudes: Were there laws written into the statutes of the nation or any subdivision of the nation that limited or restricted the full participation of Jews in any aspect of life? Could Jewish worship and Jewish religious education be carried on openly, according to the law? Was there legal discrimination against those who observed the Jewish holidays? On such matters the United States showed up fairly well from the earliest days of independence until quite recent times. Perhaps the major ground for complaint was the vigorous enforcement, in some sections of the country, of Sunday-closing laws. Such enforcement created a significant discrimination against all those who observed the Sabbath on Saturday, a class that included the Jews, though a larger part of the membership of the class was made up of Saturday-observing Christian sectarians, like Seventh-Day Adventists and Seventh-Day Baptists.

The virtual absence of discriminatory legislation does not, of course, entail the virtual absence of discrimination. Unofficial exclusions and limitations came into the picture, notoriously in the form of so-called "gentlemen's agreements." These are more difficult to pin down and to measure than are instances of official discrimination unless they are written down, as restrictive covenants, and thus brought into a public context where they are subject to legal prosecution. Unofficial discrimination of this sort has appeared frequently in the United States and is still a prevalent feature of American life, by no means always directed against the Jews or Judaism. *Numerus clausus* in the strict sense has not been official in the United States, prior to some recent administrative edicts of the federal Department of Health, Education, and

Welfare, in which "benign" quotas are introduced under the name
of "affirmative action goals." In a loose, nonofficial sense, *numerus clausus* has been common in the professions, in some forms of
corporate business, in private education, and, in greatest measure, in social life.

In spite of the increase in unofficial anti-Jewish discrimination in
some areas of American life and the suspicion of some increase in
official discrimination, the Americanization of the Jews and of
Judaism has proceeded apace, even among those who were most
victimized by whatever discrimination did exist. The measure of
Americanization cannot be entirely objective. Indeed, in many
ways, the objective factors are secondary and derivative from a
subjective factor that Politzer's analysis of comic strips makes clear.
Abie the Agent, the incarnation of the Wandering Jew, was
temporarily resting in America but subjectively felt himself to be a
stranger and a visitor. Abie the Agent could never be alienated,
because in his own mind, his own subjectivity, he was an alien; Al
Capp, given the appropriate conditions, might feel alienated
because his subjectivity is American. A stranger cannot be estranged; only one who feels himself a native can be estranged.
Only a person who feels rooted can possibly be uprooted.

That this sense of at-homeness, of a comfortable rooted belonging, should have developed among the Jews of the United States of
America is certainly not a unique emergent in Jewish experience. A
similar rooting has taken place many times in earlier Jewish history.
So recurrent has been the experience that one is tempted to speak of
a Jewish talent for naturalization in a host environment, and of the
Jewish experience in America as one more instance of the operation
of this talent. Moreover, previous Jewish history teaches that
naturalization does not preclude later deracination and estrange-
ment. That the Jews feel comfortable in a host culture does not
mean that the majorities that carry that culture will necessarily feel
comfortable with, or about, their Jewish coresidents, nor that, if
they do at any time, they will continue to do so. For that matter,
there is no certainty that the same group will continue to be the
chief carriers; and, if the carriers change, the culture will not
remain the same. The lesson of Jewish history is that the wise guest,
however much he is made to feel at home, may unpack his bags but
should always keep them close at hand for instant repacking.

Whenever and wherever in the past a rooting comparable to that in the United States has taken place, there has been some degree of mutual religious influence between Judaism and the religions of the host culture. In such situations, Judaism itself (regardless of its internal variations) becomes an alternative religious interpretation of the fundamental spiritual qualities of living in that time and place. Innovations are introduced into Judaism to express the sanctification of the new mode of life. Some of these novelties become enshrined in Judaism and thus become part of the tradition of Judaism, considered as if they had been handed down to Moses at Mount Sinai. Innovations that successfully express a living religious need persist; if the need disappears or the innovation is inadequate, or if it is merely a temporary expedient, the novelty is forgotten. So the question how the Americanization experience has modified Judaism in America is both interesting in itself and a possible indication of some of the practices or beliefs or institutional arrangements that will survive into the Judaisms of the remote future.

Judaism in America— "Kosher Style"

In the sense in which, until the end of the eighteenth century, European (and, earlier, Asian) Jewry had a communal structure, the Jews of the United States have never been organized as communities. The older form of community was a device for governing Jewish life as a unified whole, without separating religious, ethnic, economic, and other aspects. In America, the various aspects of Jewish life have developed largely in independence of each other, because in the earliest times there were few Jews, and those few adopted the organizational patterns of their Protestant hosts and coresidents, and perhaps also because of the Marrano background of the earliest arrivals. There was no superstructure to hold together and rationalize the separate parts of the infrastructure.

Instead, there was a specialization of functions on an irrational basis. American Jewish life developed an institutional division of labor between, for example, synagogues and hospitals, synagogues and orphan asylums, synagogues and cemeteries, synagogues and an ordered system for maintaining and guaranteeing proper slaughtering of meats—even, at times, between synagogues and religious education. All these various institutional expressions of the three old religious requirements of Judaism—study (*Torah*), worship (*Abodah*), and philanthropy (*Gemilut Hasadim*)—developed in competition with each other for funding and for the time and personal services of individual Jews. All the structures of Jewish life in America were parts of a free-enterprise system, as were the institutions of Protestant Christianity. As a result, in contemporary American Judaism there may be institutional marriages of convenience, but there is no centralized control and therefore no common discipline or coercive force. Even such extreme traditional instruments of control as *herem,* the ban, roughly equivalent to excommunication, have no significance whatsoever in American Judaism.

A second consequence of the absence of community structure has been that, especially in the twentieth century, many synagogues have been transformed into "synagogue centers," which more accurately might be called "community centers" (as described in the last section of chapter 5). They provide opportunities for organized social activities on many age levels from play schools to senior citizens' clubs, and for special interest groups that cross age lines. The synagogue-center is a busy place; it needs an administrator who is a good traffic manager and who is also, sometimes, the rabbi. In larger and wealthier synagogues the administrative and spiritual leadership positions are separate. The need to provide space for all these activities has led to new tendencies in synagogue architecture. Just as the comparable variety of activities in the Protestant churches has led to a sharp reduction in the amount of "sacred space"—space that would seem to most people improperly used if it housed secular groups and their activities—so the "sanctuary" in newer urban synagogue buildings has been cut down to size, with various devices for occasional enlargement. Suburban synagogues that are not faced by limitations of available building space are not under the same pressures.

In the third place, as the community in the older sense fell into desuetude, the rabbi, or, in a populous area, the several rabbis who would earlier have constituted the court of Jewish law found their activities increasingly restricted to administrative and pastoral functions. The training of rabbis continues to rest heavily on the study of the codes. Rabbinical scholarship, where it exists, is still mainly legal scholarship. But many rabbis can go through a whole

career in the service of American synagogues without having
occasion to answer questions on religious law. Although little
change has been made in rabbinical training programs, the role of
the rabbi has changed significantly; once he was professionally an
interpreter of the laws, a legist, whereas now he is professionally a
minister. Like his Protestant counterparts, the rabbi of an American
Jewish congregation visits the sick; comforts the bereaved; provides
an intermediate level of counseling between the family conclave
and the psychotherapist; represents his congregation in the broader
community by serving on the boards of local hospitals, schools,
philanthropies, and civil rights organizations, and in the Jewish
world by his activity with "defense" or Zionist organizations;
attends the meetings of American service societies, like Rotary and
Kiwanis, and comparable Jewish groups; supervises the religious
education carried on by his synagogue; participates with his reader
and music director in the planning and conduct of services; and
preaches. The modern American rabbi leads an extremely busy
and useful life, but it is not the life of the rabbi of old.

Fourth, as Judaism moved first from Asia into Europe and then
from Europe to America, it moved from host cultures in which women were socially secluded and religious practice principally a mas-
culine prerogative (as, indeed, it was in classical forms of Judaism)
into a cultural setting where women, though still by no means considered as important as men, were thought to have souls to be saved,
to have religious rights and obligations. It has been said that were it
not for the unsung part played by women in the male-dominated
churches of Europe and the United States, Christianity would not
have survived into the twentieth century. Whether this is true or an
exaggeration with regard to Christianity, the story of the synagogues of the United States gives clear testimony that the survival of
Judaism has been enormously helped, perhaps even made possible,
by the dedication, the devotion, the directed energy of American
Jewish women. Only very recently has their contribution been
acknowledged. The recognition is, as yet, by no means adequate;
too often it is grudgingly given. At the liberal end of the Jewish
spectrum, a beginning has been made by the ordination of
women and their election to important offices in denominational
organizations.

A fifth illustration of ways in which the Judaisms of the United

States have changed or are changing has to do with the religious
regulations regarding food, the whole system of *Kashrut*. Let it not
be said that this is a trivial matter in a religious context; for the
committed member of many religions religious scruples about food
are more frequently and more critically in the forefront of his mind
than theology or creed. As Kallen has noted, ''Among the items God
diversely insures is, of course, the procurement and preparation of
food. The gods participate both centrally and tangently in how we
provide, prepare, and consume what we eat and drink. And eating
and drinking, no less than being born and dying, mating and
fighting and building, are, in every society, formations of the
struggle to live and to grow in which the gods are held to play
powerful roles.''[2] Here we need not be concerned to account
historically for the complex and incoherent system presented in the
Old Testament and amplified, made more complex, and somewhat
more coherent in the rabbinical codes. The only concern here is that
kashrut is one of the central elements of practice in traditional
Jewish religious life. It is an element that in many ways tended to
enforce the social separation between Jew and non-Jew, for it is the
very mark of friendship to share with another one's meat and drink.

In the early years of Judaism in America, the synagogues assumed
responsibility for maintaining the supply of meat properly slaugh-
tered, according to the rules laid down in the rabbinic literature.
Finding a qualified and trustworthy slaughterer (*shohet*) was a
major preoccupation of the authorities of the eighteenth-century
synagogues. In the nineteenth century, however, as the number of
synagogues and of ordained rabbis increased, ritual slaughtering
became part of a laissez-faire system. Individual butchers and their
wholesale suppliers made private contracts with rabbis to supervise
their slaughtering practices. Stores, restaurants, and, later, catering
establishments displayed in their windows or on their walls certi-
ficates from this rabbi or that attesting to his having ''super-
vised'' the *kashrut* of the establishment. The old Roman question
cried out to be answered, ''Quis custodiet ipse custodes?'' Who was
to supervise the supervisor, to keep watch over the watchman? In
the absence of a communal structure nothing could be done.
Except in major centers of Jewish population, where a voluntary
consociation of rabbis tried (and still tries) to protect the Jewish

consumer from fraudulent attestations, there was no real provision
for protection. There was no guarantee that the consumer was
getting the service for which he was being systematically over-
charged.[3] Only where an official agency of state or municipal
government protected the Jewish consumer as part of its general
mandate to protect all consumers from false claims was there a
totally responsible agency supervising slaughtering practice.

Recognition by members of the Jewish public that they had no
way of validating the claims made in shop windows or on restau-
rant walls may have helped break down adherence to the rules of
kashrut. One form taken by this breakdown, short of the total
rejection of dietary laws in the Reform movement, is the retention
of some of the dietary laws in the home, as a symbol of distinctive-
ness, while the whole question is disregarded when one is eating
away from home. A more moderate form retains, even when
"eating out," the ban on certain well-known prohibited foods,
such as the flesh of the pig or shellfish, while other prohibited foods
that are not known to be prohibited by those with whom one is
likely to eat are consumed without hesitation.[4] There is no
question that adherence to *kashrut* is rapidly losing its character as
an enforcer of social separation while still retaining some force as a
mode of self-identification.[5]

What has salvaged the notion of "Jewish" food as a mode of
self-identification, the light at the end of the tunnel, is that it has
been taken over by the American food-processing industry, as have
"Italian," "Chinese" and "Black" foods. Symbolizing the change
are such advertising slogans as "You don't have to be Jewish to love
Levy's Jewish Rye bread." Many non-Jews in the United States have
learned to like the taste of some Jewish food specialities, as many
Jews have learned to enjoy the food specialties of other ethnic
groups. To meet the demands of both Jews and non-Jews, a
sub-branch of the "convenience foods" industry has grown up to
produce and to market, through supermarkets across the nation,
what are called "Kosher-style" foods. A homogenized version of a
particular taste has become a commercial substitute for the following of a complicated set of rules. Many people who do not eat
kosher, do eat kosher-style. Nostalgia as well as a sense of ethnic
solidarity can be satisfied out of a can or jar.

Perhaps many Jewish Americans in all denominations have substituted a "kosher-style" Judaism, based on a combination of ethnicity and nostalgia, for the "kosher" Judaism of their ancestors.

Religious Creativity in American Judaism

The United States has always asserted the ideal of personal freedom for its inhabitants. There has always been a gap between the asserted ideal and current practice. The theory of freedom has been spelled out in a wide variety of legal decisions, largely based upon the text of the First Amendment to the Constitution of the United States. One thing that personal freedom has always meant on the American scene has been that no official compulsion to practice a religion or even to affiliate with a religious group can be effectively exercised unless the coerced individual is ready to conform. In adult life, at least, one's religious commitments are as nearly completely voluntary as human choices can ever be. Inevitably this almost totally voluntary character of religious commitment has led to a high level of voluntary nonaffiliation with formal religious institutions among both Jews and Christians, as well as to completely voluntary conversions in both directions.

Nonaffiliation is by no means the same as nonreligion. It surely does indicate a measure of indifference to the traditional modes of expressing religious feeling in one's community. It may lead, as so often it has in the American host culture's Protestantisms, to the attempt to find new and religiously relevant ways to express contemporary religious feeling. Among Jews it may lead to serious efforts to find ways of being religiously Jewish that have personal meaning for twentieth-century Jews. At one extreme the "ignostic" humanist Jews of Birmingham, Michigan, and their brethren elsewhere exemplify this effort; at the other extreme so do those other small groups—the proper term might be "communes" or *havurot*—that are deliberately and consciously experimenting with new ritual forms as well as with new social organization of the "congregation"—organizations without superordination or subordination, without fixed religious roles, that carry to an ultimate point the democratic principle.

Groups of this sort, existing on the fringes of the various Jewish "establishments," are often anathematized by leaders of the more formally structured society. They must not be rejected, however, because they represent the continuing creative force in Judaism. Their creativity is so novel and so vital that it can be maintained only outside the traditional structures. New ideas, new inspirations, new aesthetic forms do not develop in calcified institutions, but rather in flexible, supple communities. The ease with which such groups can form, re-form, dissolve and reemerge in the voluntaristic atmosphere supported by American traditions has been a major factor in promoting the Americanization of Judaism in the United States. It is dismaying to think that there are some people who would attempt to interpret the voluntary principle written into the First Amendment in ways that would adversely affect the freedom of all Americans, including Jewish Americans, to create new ways of satisfying their spiritual needs.

Another factor in the American cultural environment that has been a source of fruitful creativity and therefore of value to Judaism is its diversity. From time to time, sometimes for political reasons, sometimes for anticipated educational benefits, but probably most often for commercial reasons, there has been an attempt in the United States to force-feed an ideal of uniformity. Such efforts have never succeeded more than temporarily, and then only in matters of lesser moment, like fashions of dress and modes of address. Always the variations and diversities in American life have again burst through the surface of artificially stimulated uniformity and have renewed the vitality of differentiation. As a consequence there has been a meeting and mutual fertilization of ethnic subcultures, but no permanent merging. Cultural pluralism in the host environment has always provided Judaism with the best medium for creativity to flourish in. With no important exception, every creative period in the history of Judaism has come at a time when, and in a place where, the Jews have been in intimate contact with other cultures. Withal, in all its millennial history, Judaism has never been in such close and sometimes even friendly contact with so many, so diverse, so religiously exciting, and so stimulating a range of religious cultures as in present-day America. Never before have the creative possibilities of Judaism been so challenged as in the United States, the haven of diversity.

Voluntaryism and pluralism, then, combine with "protestantization" to provide the possibility of a Jewish "renaissance" in the

United States. There are, however, no guarantees; voluntaryism, pluralism, and denominationalism can feed into countercreative tendencies as well as creative ones. There is as much possibility of voluntary retreat in American Jewry as there is of voluntary advance. There is as much Jewish "endarkenment" as there is Jewish "enlightenment." Voluntaryism can mean a voluntary return to the rigidities of the past or a voluntary facing of the future with courage, confidence, and creative originality. Pluralism can lead to a self-segregating insistence on the right of Judaism to be seclusive, anachronistic, and irrelevant, just as it can lead to a vital interplay with other varieties of American religious culture and a creative interchange of symbols and ideas.

The host culture is remarkably hospitable. It has manifested this in its willingness to accept the numerically small Jewish group as a third American faith. The opportunity is thus available for a vital Judaism to serve as an alternative religious interpretation of the pluralistic culture of the United States. Opportunity is also there for Judaism to turn inward, and interpret only the Jewish tradition—to become, as some of the Protestant groups have become, a sectarian enclave. The way of sectarianism leads ultimately to irrelevancy on the larger scene and thus to extinction—not extinction of the Jews, for they are indeed the Eternal People, but of Judaism, for a religion remains alive only as long as it answers adequately its adherents' questions about how to live their lives in their own time and place. The way of variety, constant novelty, fearless facing of the need for revitalizing change, can produce many heart-wrenching rejections of well-loved traditional forms and expressions. It can also bring disaster for Judaism, because a religion can overfragment and fly apart and be destroyed, even as it can be destroyed by calcifying and thus achieving a state of inanition. There is no easy answer; no slogan can shape a balance between tradition and innovation. To "re-Judaize" Judaism by "de-Americanization" will not guarantee the future of Judaism any more than to "re-Judaize" Judaism by continuing the process of Americanization.

Notes

Introduction

1.   Solomon Schechter, who built the Jewish Theological Seminary of America, in New York City, into one of the great Jewish scholarly institutions, was born in Rumania and academically trained in Germany. He taught at Cambridge University in England before coming to the United States. He also inverted the usual unthinking notion that there is an entity called "Judaism" that determines who is to be regarded as a Jew. Schechter argued that "Judaism" in any age is what the Jews of that age are willing to believe and practice. See his *Studies in Judaism: First Series* (Philadelphia, 1938; originally published in 1896), pp. xix–xx

2.   Horace M. Kallen, who coined the expression "cultural pluralism" and became its staunchest advocate, was born in Germany, brought to the United States as a young man, and trained at Harvard University in literature and philosophy. He became a major figure in social thought and was for many years professor of philosophy at the New School for Social Research in New York City. From his earliest days he had a deep interest in the cultural heritage of his Jewish ancestry; he became an ardent democrat in the United States. "Cultural pluralism," definable in some senses as the equal right of all cultural traditions to survival and expression in a democratic society, became his prescription for ethnic identity for all minorities, including the Jews.

3.   There is an extended discussion of many of these points in Joseph L. Blau, *Modern Varieties of Judaism* (New York, 1966).

4.   The term "diaspora" means "dispersion" and has been used for many centuries to designate Jewish life outside of the Holy Land. Although it is often used as a synonym for "exile," I follow a suggestion of Arthur A. Cohen, *The Natural and the Supernatural Jew: An Historical and Theological Introduction* (New York, 1962): "The Dispersion is but the historical fact. The Exile transposes that fact into a different order of apprehension, and a construct of faith emerges.... The Exile is a cosmic, not an historical, event in Jewish tradition" (pp. 182–83).

5.   Ralph Waldo Emerson, "Self-Reliance"; the quotation continues, ". . . adored by little statesmen and philosophers and divines."
6.   John A. Kouwenhoven, "What's American about America?" in his collection of essays, *The Beer Can by the Highway* (Garden City, N.Y., 1961), pp. 39-73. I owe the formulation of my section title to Kouwenhoven. Early drafts of both his essay and this section of my book were presented as papers before the Columbia University Seminar on American Civilization.
7.   Sidney E. Mead, *Lively Experiment: The Shaping of Christianity in America* (New York, 1963). Mead's book is based on his lectures on the Walgreen Foundation at the University of Chicago in 1954; I had begun to use my term "protestantism" at about the same time, independently of Mead.
8.   Samuel Hoffenstein, *Poems in Praise of Practically Nothing* (New York, 1928).
9.   E.g., Reinhold Niebuhr, in *The Nature and Destiny of Man* (New York, 1949), and his other theological works.
10.   George Foot Moore, *Judaism in the First Centuries of the Christian Era. The Age of the Tannaim*, 3 vols. (Cambridge, Mass., 1927-30).
11.   Horace M. Kallen, "*Of Them Which Say They Are Jews*" (New York, 1954), pp. 33-41; cf. The Revelation of St. John, 2:9.
12.   The Sephardic Jews are those who resided in Spain and Portugal, and, after the expulsions from these two countries at the end of the fifteenth century, their descendants in the Mediterranean countries and elsewhere. Sephardic traditional practice, pronunciation of Hebrew, and language of common use (Judeo-Spanish or Ladino) differ from those of the North and East European Jews (Ashkenazic Jews). The oldest synagogues in the United States were founded by Sephardic Jews and continue to follow Sephardic customs.
13.   See Hyman B. Grinstein, *The Rise of the Jewish Community of New York, 1654-1860* (Philadelphia, 1945), as well as David and Tamar de Sola Pool, *An Old Faith in the New World* (New York, 1955).
14.   Marshall Sklare, *Conservative Judaism: An American Religious Movement* (Glencoe, Ill., 1955), p. 46 n.

2   *Historical Sketch*

1.   There is no conclusive evidence supporting the story that Columbus was of Jewish ancestry, yet the story is widespread and often referred to. Maurice David, *Who was Columbus?* (New York, 1933), and other works of the same stripe are not to be trusted. Samuel Eliot Morison, *Admiral of the Ocean Sea: A Life of Christopher Columbus* (Boston, 1942), writes: "Columbus always loved to apply the Sacred Scriptures to his own life and adventures; it is ridiculous to read into this passage [referring to the Exodus] a secret admission of Jewish blood or an ambition to provide a new home for a persecuted race" (p. 207). This is a valid critique of the type of "evidence" often relied upon by such writers. There is, however, no final

reason here for denying the possibility of Jewish ancestry, either. See Salo W. Baron, *Steeled by Adversity: Essays and Addresses on American Jewish Life*, ed. Jeannette M. Baron (Philadelphia, 1971), p. 21; see also, on Justinian's life of Columbus, Joseph L. Blau, "An Unpublished English Translation of Justinian's Life of Columbus," *Columbia Library Columns* 12, no. 3 (1964): 9-20. The presence of Marranos in Columbus' crew and also among those who financed the initial voyage is well established; see Charles M. Segal, *Fascinating Facts about American Jewish History* (New York, 1955), pp. 13-16.

2.   For details of the early history of the Jews in New York City, see Grinstein, *The Rise of the Jewish Community of New York, 1654-1860;* David and Tamar de Sola Pool, *An Old Faith in the New World;* and, somewhat dated, but occasionally valuable, Peter Wiernik, *History of the Jews in America,* 2d ed., revised and enlarged (New York, 1931). An extended discussion of the problems of Shearith Israel in administering its cemetery properties is available in the introductory section of David de Sola Pool, *Portraits Etched in Stone: Early Jewish Settlers, 1682-1831* (New York, 1952).

3.   Texts as given in Wiernik, *History of the Jews in America,* p. 65.

4.   There are an increasing number of responsible community histories; in general the older histories were precritical, and useful chiefly for such matters as lists of members, whereas the newer histories were either written or given advisory supervision by professional historians. For Newport, see Morris A. Gutstein, *The Story of the Jews of Newport, 1658-1908* (New York, 1936); for Philadelphia, the splendid work of Edwin Wolf, 2d, and Maxwell Whiteman, *The History of the Jews of Philadelphia from Colonial Times to the Age of Jackson* (Philadelphia, 1957); for Charleston, Charles Reznikoff and Uriah Z. Engelman, *The Jew of Charleston* (Philadelphia, 1950). The early records of the Richmond congregation have been destroyed and there is no critical history, nor is there for the Savannah community.

5.   Martin Marty has pointed out (in a communication to the writer) that all the cities with a population of more than ten thousand in the colonial period were seaports, so that it may well be the urban pattern of Jewish living that is centrally involved, rather than any special relation of the Jews to international commerce. This caution is valuable; one must avoid overstating the role of Jews in large-scale international trade.

6.   See the documents in Joseph L. Blau and Salo W. Baron, *The Jews of the United States: A Documentary History, 1790-1840* (New York, 1963) 1: 70-73.

7.   On Haym Salomon, see Charles Edward Russell, *Haym Salomon and the Revolution* (New York, 1930).

8.   Blau and Baron, *The Jews of the United States* 1: 60-63.

9.   Moses Mendelssohn, *Jerusalem, oder über Religiöse Macht und Judentum* (Berlin, 1783): "Leider! hören wir auch schon den Congress in Amerika das alte Lied anstimmen, und von einer *herrschenden Religion* sprechen" (p. 140).

10.   See the interesting documents collected by Rudolf Glanz,

"Source Materials on the History of Jewish Immigration to the United States, 1800–1880," *YIVO Annual of Jewish Social Science* 4 (1951).
11.   Grinstein, *Rise of the Jewish Community of New York*, pp. 91, 233 ff., 395–998, and the documents in his Appendix XI, pp. 513–17.
12.   Quoted from the minutes of Congregation Beth Elohim by Joseph Buchler, "The Struggle for Unity: Attempts at Union in American Jewish Life," *American Jewish Archives* 2 (1949–50): 27.
13.   Henry S. Morais, *The Jews of Philadelphia* (Philadelphia, 1894), pp. 89–90.
14.   Moshe Davis, "Jewish Religious Life and Institutions in America," in *The Jews,* ed., Louis Finkelstein (New York, 1949), 1: 366.
15.   *The Occident,* 6 (1848–49): 431–33.
16.   Ibid., 430.
17.   *The Occident,* 7 (1849–50): 63.
18.   The older account, in David Philipson, *The Reform Movement in Judaism* (1907; new and revised ed., 1930; reissued with an introduction by Solomon B. Freehof, New York, 1967) is still of some value. Extremely useful, though fragmentary, sources are collected in W. Gunther Plaut, ed., *The Rise of Reform Judaism* (New York, 1963) and *The Growth of Reform Judaism* (New York, 1965). See also Blau, *Modern Varieties of Judaism,* chap. 2, for a brief overview of the development of Reform Judaism. The entire text of the Charleston petition of 1824 is reprinted in Blau and Baron, *The Jews of the United States* 2: 554–60.
19.   Blau and Baron, *The Jews of the United States* 2: 560.
20.   *The Occident* 1 (1843–44): 157–61; 217–30.
21.   This attack was originally published in Isaac M. Wise's paper, *The Israelite,* of which Lilienthal was Corresponding Editor. It is given here as reprinted by Leeser in *The Occident* 14 (1856–57): 380–81.
22.   *The Jewish Messenger,* 23 October 1857.
23.   It has been said that a large number of Jewish "48ers" came to the United States. Leon A. Jick, in "Jews in the Synagogue—Americans Everywhere: The German-Jewish Immigration and the Emergence of the American Jewish Pattern, 1820–1870" (Ph.D. diss., Columbia University, 1973), completely disproves this filio-pietistic myth.
24.   See Joseph L. Blau, "An American-Jewish View of the Evolution Controversy," *Hebrew Union College Annual* 20 (1947): 617–34.
25.   The lectures were published in 1887 by Berkowitz and Company of Kansas City, under the title *Evolution and Judaism.*
26.   Krauskopf, *Evolution and Judaism,* p. 284.
27.   Ibid., pp. 308–9.
28.   Ibid., pp. 297–99.
29.   This series of Kohut's sermons was published (belatedly) under the title *The Ethics of the Fathers* (New York, 1920); for a view of the controversy by a later adherent of the Conservative position, see Moshe Davis, *The Emergence of Conservative Judaism: The Historical School in 19th Century America* (Philadelphia, 1963), pp. 222–28; for the view of a Reform rabbinical scholar, see Albert H. Friedlander, "Reform Judaism in

America: The Pittsburgh Platform" (mimeographed; New York: Union of American Hebrew Congregations, 1958), pp. 13 ff.

30.   *Proceedings of the Pittsburgh Rabbinical Conference, November 16, 17, 18, 1885.* Published by the Central Conference of American Rabbis in honor of . . . Rabbi Kaufmann Kohler . . ., 1923, p. 6.

31.   Ibid., pp. 7–8.

32.   The full text is reprinted in ibid., pp. 24–25.

33.   Mordecai M. Kaplan, *The Religion of Ethical Nationhood* (New York, 1970), p. 13.

34.   See Herbert Parzen, "When Secularism Came to Russian Jewry," *Commentary,* April 1952, pp. 355–62.

35.   J. D. Eisenstein, "The History of the First Russian-American Jewish Congregation, The Beth Hamedrosh Hagodol," reprinted in *The Jewish Experience in America: Selected Studies from the Publications of the American Jewish Historical Society,* ed. Abraham J. Karp (Waltham, Mass., and New York, 1969) 3: 140.

36.   Eisenstein's article (see n. 35 above) reports in detail the history of the early days of this congregation.

37.   Charles S. Liebman, "Orthodoxy in American Jewish Life," *American Jewish Yearbook* 66 (1965): 29. Among the citations in Liebman's note to this point is the following quotation from Milton Himmelfarb, "The Intellectual and the Rabbi," *Proceedings of the Rabbinical Assembly of America* 1963, p. 124: "After all, who went to America? Overwhelmingly it was not the elite of learning, piety, or money but the *shnayders* [tailors], the *shusters* [cobblers], and the *ferd-ganovim* [horse thieves]."

38.   The term was used by the secretary to the outstanding rabbinical authority of Russia at that time; see Abraham J. Karp, "New York Chooses a Chief Rabbi," *Publications of the American Jewish Historical Society* 44 (1954–55): 129–98.

39.   Among the Chinese immigrants to the United States, a sense of family superiority (often found among other groups as well, including the Jews) took the place of the *shtetl*-superiority discussed here. Much of what is called "Black anti-Semitism" in the United States today is an expression of the need to feel superior to someone. Consider, too, the conflict of national groups within the Roman Catholic Church, and the perpetuation of national distinctions in the various Lutheran Church bodies in America.

40.   Moshe Davis, "Jewish Religious Life and Institutions in America," 1: 405.

41.   *The Occident* 22 (1863–64): 61.

3   Twentieth-Century
                                          Alternatives

1.   Robert Lyon in *The Asmonean,* 2 January 1852; Kaufmann Kohler, in *Jewish Theology Systematically and Historically Considered* (New York, 1918; reprinted, with introduction by J. L. Blau, New York,

1968), p. vii; on change and permanence, see Morris Raphael Cohen, *Reason and Nature* (New York, 1931), pp. 18–19.

2.   Gotthard Deutsch, *Scrolls: Essays on Jewish History and Literature and Kindred Subjects* (New York, 1917) 1: 97.

3.   See *Shulhan Arukh, Hoshen Mishpat*, 17, 3. The *Shulhan Arukh* by Joseph Caro, with annotations by Moses Isserles, is an authoritative code of Jewish law produced in the sixteenth century.

4.   Deutsch, *Scrolls* 1: 96. The "days of awe" (*yamim noraim*) are the major Holy Days of modern Judaism: the New Year (*rosh hashana*), and the Day of Atonement (*yom kippur*), together with the intervening ten "penitential days."

5.   See, in addition, Ray Schultz, "The Call of the Ghetto," *New York Times Magazine,* 10 November 1974, pp. 34, 113–21, 129.

6.   See Ellis Rivkin, *The Shaping of Jewish History* (New York, 1971) for a comparable view, stressing the impact of world cultures on the Jews, but emphasizing more than I the uniqueness and individuality of Jewish history. "Jewish historical experience," says Rivkin, "... is rather interlocked with the emergence and development of Western civilization—a minority interlocking in reciprocal interaction with large, complex, and enveloping cultures, societies, and civilizations. For though each phase of Jewish history bears the stamp of the enveloping society, it is, nonetheless, highly differentiated from it. Its individuality *is* the outcome of successive interactions with the encompassing culture, society, or civilization" (quoted in Michael A. Meyer, *Ideas of Jewish History* [New York, (c. 1974)], pp. 338–39). The expression "failure of nerve," as I have used it here, is borrowed from Sidney Hook, who uses it to indicate a parallel between the twentieth-century shrinking into various forms of obscurantism as a reaction against the earlier triumphs of modern science and the retreat of the Hellenistic Age into a variety of salvational cults, as described by Gilbert Murray in his *Five Stages of Greek Religion* (Oxford, 1925), where the expression was first published.

7.   Abraham J. Feldman, *The American Reform Rabbi: A Profile of a Profession* (New York, 1965), pp. 45–46. The *esrog* or *ethrog* is a citron; the *lulav* or *lulab* is a palm branch; they are used together ceremonially in the ritual of the Feast of Booths (*sukkoth*), the harvest festival.

8.   See the examples in J. L. Blau, ed., *Reform Judaism: A Historical Perspective* (New York, 1973), pp. 304–47.

9.   Ibid., p. 18.

10.   J. L. Blau, *Modern Varieties of Judaism,* pp. 91–95; a fuller treatment may be found in Louis Ginzberg, *Students, Scholars, and Saints* (Philadelphia, 1928), pp. 195–216.

11.   Solomon Schechter, *Seminary Addresses and Other Papers* (Cincinnati, 1915), p. viii.

12.   Solomon Schechter, *Studies in Judaism: First Series,* p. xix.

13.   Solomon Schechter, *Studies in Judaism. Second Series* (Philadelphia, 1908), p. 116.

14.   Near the end of his life, Schechter wrote, "I still belong to that older world which accepted certain humanitarian principles handed down to us from the French Revolution as God-given truths, and which still looks upon the 'Declaration of Independence,' based on the same principles, as a sacred document in spite of all its 'glittering generalities.' These 'glittering generalities' have built up the new world, while the so-called 'eternal verities' or 'realities' are destroying the old world" (*Seminary Addresses*, p. xi). Even allowing for the fact that this was written during the earlier half of World War I, it does show the continuing impact of the Enlightenment on Schechter.

15.   Jacob Neusner, "Conservative Judaism in a Divided Community," *Conservative Judaism* 20 (1965-66), no. 4, pp. 1-2.

16.   Marshall Sklare, *Conservative Judaism*, pp. 159-98. This chapter deals with the "Conservative rabbi." Four of the seven subheads include the words "discontinuities and conflicts."

17.   Milton Steinberg, *A Partisan Guide to the Jewish Problem* (Indianapolis, [c. 1945]), p. 166.

18.   Mordecai M. Kaplan, *The Purpose and Meaning of Jewish Existence: A People in the Image of God* (Philadelphia, 1964), p. 299.

19.   Mordecai M. Kaplan, "The Way I Have Come," in *Mordecai M. Kaplan: An Evaluation*, ed. Ira Eisenstein and Eugene Kohn (New York, 1952), p. 296.

20.   Ibid., pp. 301-8.

21.   Mordecai M. Kaplan, *Judaism as a Civilization: Toward a Reconstruction of American Jewish Life* (1934; reprinted New York, 1957), p. 345.

22.   For both quotations, see *The Purpose and Meaning of Jewish Existence*, p. 311.

23.   This much is clear from the genealogical studies of Malcolm Stern. See his major work, *Americans of Jewish Descent* (Cincinnati, 1960), as well as such specialized articles as his "Jewish Marriage and Intermarriage in the Federal Period," *American Jewish Archives* 19 (1967): 142-43.

24.   On this group, see Ernest Stock, "Washington Heights' 'Fourth Reich,' " *Commentary*, June 1951, pp. 581-88.

25.   Charles S. Liebman, 'Orthodoxy in American Jewish Life," p. 21.

26.   Sklare, *Conservative Judaism*, p. 46.

27.   Liebman, "Orthodoxy in American Jewish Life," pp. 34-36.

28.   Ibid., p. 31.

29.   Ibid., p. 38.

30.   Thus, for example, the anticultic passages in the pre-Exilic prophets in the Old Testament surely evidence the emergence of a new sense of spirituality.

4   *Zionism as a
Religious Experience*

1.   Samuel H. Levine, "Palestine in the Literature of the United States to 1867," and Milton Plesur, "The American Press and Jewish Restoration during the Nineteenth Century," both in *Early History of Zionism in America*, ed. Isidore S. Meyer (American Jewish Historical Society and Theodor Herzl Foundation, New York, 1958), pp. 21–28 and 55–76. See also, Moshe Davis' remarks in opening the first session of the colloquium *America and the Holy Land* (published by the Institute of Contemporary Jewry of the Hebrew University of Jerusalem, 1972), p. 5.

2.   The text of Robinson's proposal, with introductory comment, is available in Joseph L. Blau and Salo W. Baron, eds., *The Jews of the United States* 3:878–84.

3.   See Blau and Baron, *The Jews of the United States* 3:878.

4.   On Noah and his plans, see Blau and Baron, *The Jews of the United States* 3:885–905; A. B. Makover, *Mordecai M. Noah* (New York, 1917); and Isaac Goldberg, *Major Noah: American-Jewish Pioneer* (Philadelphia, 1936).

5.   Isaac Leeser, *Discourses, Argumentative and Devotional* (Philadelphia, 1837); sections of this address on restoration to Zion are reprinted in Blau and Baron, *The Jews of the United States* 3:912–16. See also "The Jewish Creed," in *The Occident* 1 (1843–44): 157–61, where Leeser insists editorially on the teaching of the literal coming of the Messiah and the resurrection of the dead.

6.   *The Occident,* 11 (1853–54): 434.

7.   Ibid., p. 478.

8.   See Abraham J. Karp, "The Zionism of Warder Cresson," in Meyer, ed., *Early History of Zionism in America,* pp. 1–20.

9.   *The Occident,* 11 (1853–54): 487. .

10.   Quoted by Karp (see n. 8), p. 4 from the ms. in the National Archives.

11.   Thackeray's account of his visit to Cresson appears in his "Notes of a Journey from Cornhill to Grand Cairo" and may be found in any complete edition of the author's works. Other documentation is available in Karp's article (see note 8), and in the literature referred to by Karp.

12.   Quoted from Warder Cresson's *The Key of David. . . .* (Philadelphia, 1852), p. 205, by Karp (see note 8), p. 7.

13.   Karp (see note 8), p. 9.

14.   Details of the history of this group are available in Joseph Bluestone's memoirs and scrapbook, presented in summary by Hyman B. Grinstein in the *Publications of the American Jewish Historical Society* 35 (1939). See also Shlomo Noble, "Pre-Herzlian Zionism in America as Reflected in the Yiddish Press," in Meyer, ed., *Early History of Zionism in America,* pp. 39–54, suggesting that the generally accepted date of 1882, based on Grinstein, is a misinterpretation and should be 1884.

15. See Bernard Richards, "Zionism in the United States," a supplementary chapter in the American edition of Israel Cohen, *The Zionist Movement* (New York, 1946). Richards, who wrote this chapter in extreme old age, was a belated survivor of the activists of the nineteenth-century group.

16. Anita Liebman Lebeson, "Zionism Comes to Chicago," in Meyer, ed., *Early History of Zionism in America*, pp. 155-90. Indications of the most frequent early response of the Reform movement to Zionism may be found in Joseph L. Blau, ed., *Reform Judaism*, pp. 367-436.

17. See the discussion in Joseph L. Blau, *Modern Varieties of Judaism*, chap. 5, especially, on this point, pp. 145-47.

18. Zionism was, indeed, almost too central, for many people. In the earliest days of Israel's independence, a neighbor of mine shifted his affiliation from a Conservative to an Orthodox synagogue. His explanation was that in the rabbi's sermons on the High Holy Days (*yamim noraim*), a great deal was said about Israel, but very little about God. My neighbor was unwittingly pointing to the important caution that idolatry remains a temptation and a danger, even in modern religion.

19. Oscar and Mary Handlin, "A Century of Jewish Immigration to the United States," *American Jewish Yearbook* 50 (1948-49): 78.

20. Israel Goldstein, *Towards a Solution* (New York, 1940), p. 176.

21. The "call" was widely reprinted. As given here, the quotation is excerpted from the full text as printed in the Atlantic City, N.J., *Jewish Record*, 2 April 1948.

22. An instance worthy of this special note is that of Rabbi Meir Kahane, founder of the Jewish Defense League, whose activities in Israel have constituted such embarrassment to the Israeli government that he was, for a time, held in custody. Yet to the naïve eyes of many (if not most) American Jews, Kahane and his followers are carrying out a strong pro-Israel policy.

23. Marshall Sklare, *America's Jews* (New York, 1971), p. 221.

5   *Individual*   *Affiliation*
   and Community: *and Disaffiliation*

1. See Blau and Baron, *The Jews of the United States*, 3: 688, for details of the Masonic procession in connection with the dedication of the synagogue of Congregation Mickve Israel of Savannah, Georgia, in 1820: "It being an established custom whenever a public Edifice and particularly a place of worship is to be erected, that a Masonic procession is most commonly invited. . . . Taking it then for granted that this measure will be adopted, The Hebrew Bretheren [sic] will attend at the Grand Lodge Room. The other Israelites who are not Masons will assemble at some adjacent place in order to fall in with the procession."

2. A full historical discussion is to be found in Salo W. Baron, *The*

Jewish Community: Its History and Structure to the American Revolution,
3 vols. (Philadelphia, 1942).

3.   This statement, on the surface, may sound unduly extreme. We
may think, however, of the father of Hamlin Garland, who thought it was
time to pick up stakes and move farther to the west when he was able to
stand in front of his cabin and see the smoke rising from his neighbor's
chimney. The father of the poet Robert P. Tristram Coffin moved his
family from place to place in Maine, and finally to a small island off the
coast, cut off from the mainland for six months of the year, in order to get
away from having neighbors.

4.   See, for example, the correspondence between members of the
Mailert (Meylert) family, in Blau and Baron, *The Jews of the United States*
3:807-24.

5.   See Oscar and Mary F. Handlin, "The Acquisition of Political
and Social Rights by the Jews in the United States," *American Jewish
Yearbook* 56 (1955): 70-80; note especially the Handlins' comments
distinguishing upper-class "longings for exclusive, quasi-aristocratic status" (p. 72), leading to a policy of social exclusion of Jews; professional
"fear of competition and uncertainty as to whether there really would be
enough room for everyone" (p. 76), leading to the restriction of Jewish
admissions to professional schools; and a "still more virulent form of
anti-Semitism" that "began to take form in the 1890s among social groups
that were experiencing tensions quite different from those which troubled
the would-be aristocracy" (p. 78), such as the farmers and the working
classes and the many adherents of the various forms of Populism which
were embraced by the farmers and laborers. See also John Higham,
Strangers in the Land: Patterns of American Nativism, 1860-1925 (1955;
Atheneum ed., New York, 1963), especially pp. 92-94; Higham regards
the anti-Semitism of the 1890s as more substantially ideological than I do.

6.   For a brief statement of Kaplan's program, see Mordecai M.
Kaplan, *Judaism in Transition* (New York, 1926), Appendix I, pp. 301-6.
See also *Mordecai M. Kaplan: An Evaluation,* ed. Ira Eisenstein and
Eugene Kohn (New York, 1952) for essays by Samuel Dinin, Samuel C.
Kohs, and Louis Kraft, commenting from their various viewpoints on
Kaplan's ideas for the Jewish community.

7.   Israel Goldstein, "The Menace of Secularism in the Synagogue,"
*Proceedings of the Twenty-ninth Annual Convention of the Rabbinical
Assembly of the Jewish Theological Seminary of America* (1929), p. 94.
The words of David Aronson are cited from the report in The Indianapolis
Jewish Post, 24 June 1949. Twenty-five years earlier, in 1924, Rabbi Joel
Blau had defined a synagogue-center slightingly as "a *shul* with a pool."

8.   Mordecai M. Kaplan, "Need Rabbi and Social Worker Clash?"
Opinion, 28 March 1932: "Opportunity has brought to the Rabbi the
institution of the Jewish Center. If he had only known how to utilize it, he
could have made of it the means to be a Jewish spiritual and cultural
renaissance."

6   *Jew and Non-Jew:*   *The Problem of Pluralism*

1.   See Joshua Trachtenberg, *The Devil and the Jews* (New Haven, Conn., 1943) for a classic study of the superstitious attitudes of medieval Christians toward the Jews.

2.   The story of Joseph Jonas and the Quaker lady is repeated in Charles M. Segal, *Fascinating Facts about American Jewish History,* pp. 65-66. One of my daughters had the experience of being stared at from the doorway of her dormitory room at a great midwestern university. I myself once sat at a table with a group of advanced seminarians at a Jesuit seminary. With one exception all had been born in the United States. Only one of them had come from an urban background, and he was the only one to have had any previous contact at the social level with a Jew.

3.   Presented in his book, *Protestant, Catholic, Jew* (New York, 1955). Will Herberg is often incorrectly spoken of as an advocate of the three-faith America, rather than as its analyst.

4.   More than family—*mishpoche*. It has been well said that one may find "a banker at Bankers Trust" and "a friend at Chase Manhattan"; at the Bank of Israel one finds a relative.

5.   The old American Jewish joke is pathetically apposite: A young Jewish mother was wheeling her two young sons along the Grand Concourse, in the Bronx, in New York City, when an older acquaintance stopped her, admired the boys, and asked their ages. The mother replied, "The doctor on the right is two and a half; the lawyer on the left is eight months old."

6.   In part, what is said here is intended as a response to the brilliant, but somehow wrongheaded, treatment by William Carey McWilliams, *The Idea of Fraternity in America* (Berkeley, Calif., 1973), notably pp. 496-98. McWilliams' special pleading shows clearly when he speaks of "the very dubious concept of 'black anti-Semitism' " (p. 498). Of recent times, this author asserts, "Organization and organized action among Jews greatly expanded. Yet this development only checked deculturation, it did not halt or reverse it. Increased ethnic identification has not necessarily implied devotion to Judaic culture" (p. 497). If by "culture" one means "culchah (loud cheers!)," McWilliams is surely justified. In the more social-scientific meaning of the term, however, I suggest that he needs to reconsider; American culture has become Judaized at the same rate that Jewish culture has become Americanized.

7.   Samuel Oppenheim, *The Jews and Masonry in the United States before 1810,* pp. 5-8. This pamphlet is an offprint from vol. 19 of the *Publications of the American Jewish Historical Society.* See also the letters of David Nathans to his father, in Joseph L. Blau and Salo W. Baron, eds., *The Jews of the United States* 3:697-700.

8.   Ossian Lang, *History of Freemasonry in the State of New York* (New York, 1922), p. 38.

9.   Julius Bien, "A History of the Independent Order Bnai Brith," as quoted in Hyman B. Grinstein, *The Rise of the Jewish Community of New York, 1654-1860* (Philadelphia, 1945), p. 462. It is worth adding that a very important social club for German Jews in midtown New York City was named the Harmonie Club.

10.   Charles H. Brigham, "The Progressive Jews: A Christian View," *The Golden Age*, April 1871, reprinted in the *Jewish Times*, 5 May 1871.

11.   See Charles S. Liebman, "Orthodoxy in American Jewish Life," pp. 87-88, for a brief and informed discussion of Rabbi Joseph Soloveitchik's role in modern Orthodox circles; especially worth noting is Liebman's judgment that "The Rov [i.e., Soloveitchik] may be the leader of modern Orthodoxy, but he is not really modern Orthodox."

12.   *New York Herald Tribune*, January 26, 1966, p. 18.

13.   The old story of the minister who, after heated debate with a colleague about a minor theological point, said, "Let us not argue further; let us part in peace, you to worship God in your way, I to worship Him in His way," is all too painfully appropriate. So, too, is the report that during the debate on the Test Acts in the British House of Lords in the mid-eighteenth century, one of the lords whispered to Bishop William Warburton, "I have heard much, my Lord Bishop, of orthodoxy and heterodoxy; what do these words mean?" The bishop whispered in reply, "Orthodoxy, my Lord, orthodoxy is my doxy; heterodoxy is another man's doxy." Joseph Priestley, *Memoirs* 1:572.

14.   Horace M. Kallen, *Cultural Pluralism and the American Idea. An Essay in Social Philosophy* (Philadelphia, 1956), p. 98.

7   *The Americanization
                                     of American Judaism*

1.   Heinz Politzer, "From Little Nemo to Li'l Abner," in *The Funnies: An American Idiom*, ed. David Manning White and Robert H. Abel (Glencoe, Illinois, 1963), p. 48.

2.   Horace Kallen, *Cultural Pluralism*, p. 30. See also Marshall Sklare, *America's Jews*: "The dietary laws are a striking illustration of Judaism's sacramental tradition. They invest the routine and mundane act of eating with sacred significance and they provide the believer with recurring opportunities to show his obedience to God's will. . . . Furthermore, their observance affects the individual in the most profound ways. Observance of the laws may influence choice of friends, neighborhood, occupation, and spouse. Finally, they give the home an indisputably Jewish character" (p. 113).

3.   Charles S. Liebman, in "Orthodoxy in American Jewish Life," wrote: "The issue which most severely damaged the image" of the member rabbis of the Union of Orthodox Rabbis of the United States and Canada "was *kashrut* supervision. Rightly or wrongly, an image persisted

of the communal rabbi who, pressured by butchers, food processors, and slaughterers to ease *kashrut* requirements, and plagued by the indifference of Jewish consumers, lowered his standards of supervision" (p. 33). See also Harold O. Gastwirt, *Fraud, Corruption, and Holiness: The Controversy over the Supervision of Dietary Practice in New York City* (Port Washington, N.Y., 1972).

4.   Marshall Sklare, in *Conservative Judaism,* quotes one respondent to the question of the role of dietary laws among Conservative Jews: "I enjoy [eating] everything out that I don't have in my house, which is strictly Orthodox" (p. 204).

5.   Sklare, *Conservative Judaism,* also points out that the "really significant facts are that (1) the *isolating* function of the dietary laws no longer operates as far as most of Conservative Jewry is concerned; (2) nevertheless the role of *kashruth* as an axis of *Jewishness* is still manifest" (p. 203; italics in the original). Arthur Hertzberg, "The American Jew and His Religion," in *The American Jew: A Reappraisal,* ed. Oscar I. Janowsky (Philadelphia, 1964), writing ten years after Sklare, notes that "Obedience to the dietary laws, which are mandatory among both the Orthodox and the Conservative, has declined disastrously. A study of the most committed element of the Conservative laity, the members of the boards of congregations, has demonstrated that even in such circles no more than one in three keep completely *kosher* homes. American Orthodoxy is substantially more obedient in this area, but even among this element one-third does not observe *kashrut*" (p. 102).

Index